THE ECONOMIES
OF KAZAKSTAN
AND UZBEKISTAN

The Former Soviet South project is sponsored by:

- A. Meredith Jones & Co. Ltd.
- B.A.T Industries plc
- British Gas plc
- The British Petroleum Company plc
- ENI S.p.A.
- Mobil Oil Company Ltd
- Shell International Petroleum Company Ltd
- Statoil

Series editor: Edmund Herzig
Head, Russia and Eurasia Programme: Roy Allison

FORMER SOVIET SOUTH PROJECT

THE ECONOMIES
OF KAZAKSTAN
AND UZBEKISTAN

Michael Kaser

THE ROYAL INSTITUTE OF
INTERNATIONAL AFFAIRS
Russia and Eurasia Programme

Published in Great Britain in 1997 by the Royal Institute of International Affairs,
Chatham House, 10 St James's Square, London SW1Y 4LE
(Charity Registration No. 208 223)

Distributed worldwide by The Brookings Institution, 1775 Massachusetts Avenue, NW,
Washington, DC 20036-2188, USA.

ISBN 1 899658 55 6

Printed and bound in Great Britain by the Chameleon Press Ltd
Cover design by Youngs Design in Production

CONTENTS

Tables:

ABOUT THE AUTHOR

Professor Michael Kaser is an Emeritus Fellow of St Antony's College and Reader Emeritus in Economics of the University of Oxford; he holds an Honorary Chair of the University of Birmingham in its Institute for German Studies and is associated with its Centre for Russian and East European Studies. He has been General Editor of the International Economic Association since 1986 (and member of its Executive from 1974). Until September 1993 he was Director of the Institute of Russian, Soviet and East European Studies at Oxford. He is Chairman of the Former Soviet South Project Advisory Board of the Royal Institute of International Affairs.

After graduation in economics at King's College, Cambridge, his early career in HM Foreign Service (including HM Embassy, Moscow) and then in the United Nations Economic Commission for Europe, Geneva enabled him to take part in missions to all East European states and the Soviet Union, including Central Asia. Since 1992 he has participated in three missions of international or academic institutions to the Asian Union Republics. He is author and/or editor of 24 books and 290 articles in journals on the East European, Russian and Central Asian economies, both under the Soviet-type system and in transition to the market. In 1995–6 the Brookings Institution for the RIIA published his *Privatization in the CIS* and (with S. Mehrotra) *The Central Asian Economies after Independence*, earlier versions of which were originally published in the RIIA's Post-Soviet Business Forum series.

ACKNOWLEDGMENTS

Thanks are particularly due to members of a Study Group at the Royal Institute of International Affairs on 28 November 1996 for comments at the meeting and very promptly after it; those by Geoffrey Bray, Simon Butt, Sir Bryan Cartledge and John Slate were especially helpful. Ann Cropper's administration of the Former Soviet South Project has been both efficacious and courteous. The help of the following (some of whom were also discussants at the study group) is most appreciatively acknowledged: Alexander Agafonoff; Shirin Akiner; Roy Allison; Gregory Andrusz; Tim Ash; Annette Bohr; Helen Boss; Erik Dosmukamedou; Edmund Herzig; Shazkat Ibragimoff; Yelena Kalyuzhnova; Greg Kaser; Akira Miyamoto; Paul Rayment; Yaacov Ro'i.

December 1996   M.K.

SUMMARY

Kazakstan and Uzbekistan are not only geographically at the centre of Eurasia but at the median point of world economies, for in per capita output there are almost as many states poorer than them as there are states richer. Three characteristics emerge from this mid-point position. First, being landlocked and remote from the export markets for their oil, gas, metals and cotton, they depend on other countries for transit. In the Soviet period their southern and eastern neighbours were all but closed to their trade for there was neither political affinity nor transport infrastructure; only now are the relations and through routes being opened. Since the breakup of the USSR in late 1991 railway links have been established east to China and the Pacific Ocean and south to Iran and the Indian Ocean. The Caspian Pipeline Consortium agreement, finally signed in November 1996, will allow Kazak oil to reach the Black Sea, while Uzbek and Kazak gas is fed into the Russian domestic and export network. Further export expansion for hydrocarbons demands heavy investment and the maintenance of competitive costs of extraction and shipment. The same requirement for comparative advantage is imposed for exporting non-ferrous, rare and precious metals, which both countries, but especially Kazakstan, are fostering with foreign capital inflow and joint ventures.

The second characteristic suggested by the World Bank's ranking – the two states are almost at the bottom of the Bank's 'lower middle-income' group – is that they combine aspects of both high and low human and economic development. They are high because the labour force is better educated than in developing economies at similar income levels, and has a well-skilled core, which facilitates the transfer of sophisticated technology. Kazakstan has been harder hit than Uzbekistan by the collapse of the command economy, of military production, of Comecon and of the USSR, but both governments have kept at bay mass unemployment and poverty. Both states are low in development because they rely heavily on agriculture – the Kazak grain and Uzbek cotton crops have declined sharply since independence – and after six decades of collective and state farming tenants have not yet been granted freehold with the incentives and savings that could bring. Neither constitution permits dual nationality, and heavy Slav emigration has been a temporary hindrance to development by thinning out technical and professional staffs; replacements are being trained (current, but not capital, spending on education has held up) and the privatization of small entities (retailing, crafts and services) has released motivations for growth and the satisfaction of consumer demand that had previously been stifled. Thirdly, because both economies are medium-developed, they are attractive to foreign investors because they are capable of absorbing the practice and technology of major transnational corporations. Institutionally, that absorption is being facilitated by the implantation of market structures – notably a large, though not yet dominant, private sector – and financial services, albeit with weak banking, but is hindered by corruption and bureaucracy. Private enterprises by mid-1996 generated in each country some two-fifths of aggregate product, and included foreign majority partnerships with state firms; such joint operations may conform more readily to an authoritarian government than might independent domestic industrialists and financiers.

Consumer-driven import penetration, and the multiplication of non-state transactors (including the so-called 'shuttle-traders', who personally bring in goods from Turkey, India and East Asia), have helped to shift the direction of trade away from the 'traditional' partners of the former Soviet Union. In 1995, for the first time, Uzbekistan showed more than half its trade with 'non-traditional' countries; the Kazakstan share was then 44 per cent, but on a rising trend. Russia remains the leading partner for both.

Foreign investors and traders are attracted by prospects for political and macroeconomic stability. After overcoming the 1992 shocks of price liberalization, loss of Soviet central subsidies to the Union Republics, and later withdrawal of the 'free rider' rouble, the two countries established separate currencies – the Kazak tenge and the Uzbek sum, the former with, the latter initially without, the advice of the International Monetary Fund. IMF and World Bank counsel has continued and is supported by credits. The countries have assistance from the European Union and UN Development Programme (UNDP), and have been negotiating with these and other agencies, and also among the Central Asian states, about the reversal of environmental and ecological damage, notably to the Aral and Caspian Seas and to farmland. Until about 1994 Kazakstan was more favoured for direct inward investment than Uzbekistan, but the latter has since been eroding that lead. During 1996 each government caused foreign interests some concern – the one by a mishandled gold concession, the other by a reimposition of arbitrary foreign-exchange rationing.

The two presidential prospectuses – Kazakstan's 'Action Programme for the Deepening of Reforms' and Uzbekistan's 'Own Model for Transition to a Market Economy' – stress gradual change in the economic system based upon existing political structures.

I NATURAL AND HUMAN RESOURCES

The two economies in space and time

The neighbouring republics of Kazakstan and Uzbekistan occupy most of the resources and people of Central Asia: their combined area of 3,164,000 sq. km constitutes 79 per cent of the group of five states; their population of 39 million comprises 73 per cent; and in 1994 their GNP, estimated at purchasing power parities (PPP) as in Table 1 overleaf, was 79 per cent of that generated by the five. In the context of the Commonwealth of Independent States (CIS) other than Russia, the $100 billion GNP of the two republics compares with $244 billion generated by the other eight; on the same basis, Russia generated $684 billion. These are small aggregates against the size of the big European economies – the UK generated $1,049 million and Germany $1,588 million – but the potential for growth is there, initially in overcoming the deformities of Soviet-type planning and the post-communist recession, and in exploiting rich oil, gas and mineral deposits. These can be competitive enough for both exports and capital inflow – given continued political stability and the appropriate business environment; the recycling of such funds into domestic investment and consumption offers their citizens a prospect of substantial welfare gains.

Export earnings from natural resources depend, however, on getting the products to market, and both states are in the heart of the world's largest land mass: Uzbekistan shares with tiny Liechtenstein the distinction of being the only landlocked country surrounded by other landlocked countries. Turning that geography to advantage, President Islam Karimov speaks of 'the good historical fortune for Uzbekistan to be located on the crossroads of major routes in Central Asia. This opens up opportunities for the implementation of the general strategy ... to build an economic and cultural bridge between Europe and Asia and create favourable conditions within its framework for the exchange of goods, technologies, investments and cultural values.'[1]

[1] Islam Karimov, *Building the Future: Uzbekistan – Its Own Model for Transition to a Market Economy,* Uzbekistan Publishers, Tashkent, 1993, p. 83.

1

Table 1: Comparative economic performance in the CIS since independence

CIS state	GNP per capita PPP in 1994 ($)	Total GNP at PPP in 1994 ($ mn)	GNP as per cent of CIS in 1994	GDP in 1996 1989 = 100 (index)
Armenia	2,160	7,990	0.8	40
Azerbaijan	1,510	11,375	1.1	36
Belarus	4,320	44,930	4.4	58
Georgia	1,160*	6,265	0.6	20
Kazakstan	2,810	47,210	4.6	46
Kyrgyzstan	1,730	7,785	0.8	51
Moldova	2,450*	10,535	1.0	39
Russia	4,610	683,665	66.5	53
Tajikistan	970	5,625	0.5	37
Turkmenistan	2,990*	13,155	1.3	60
Ukraine	2,620	135,980	13.2	43
Uzbekistan	2,370	53,090	5.2	82
CIS	3,600	1,027,605	100.0	52

Sources: Col. 1 from World Bank, *World Development Report 1996* (except for asterisked estimates) and col. 4 from European Bank for Reconstruction and Development (EBRD), *Transition Report 1996*, Table 8.1 (Annex 8.1 of which gives variant estimates of GDP at PPP). Conversion at purchasing power parity (PPP) is at the number of units of the country's currency that would be needed to buy the same amount of goods and services as one dollar would buy in the United States; the CIS mean in col. 4 is, however, calculated on weights at nominal exchange rates. The CIS mean in col.1 (per capita GDP at PPP) is col. 2 divided by 285.4 mn population. Col. 2 is the product of col. 1 for each republic and population estimates in the World Bank source; col. 3 is the same as rounded percentages. Col. 4 is EBRD forecasts for 1996 of GNP (which differs from GDP by net factor income from abroad).

With a common frontier from near the Caspian Sea to the foothills of the Central Asian *massif*, the two states form a geographic zone of four parts. The steppe and forest-steppe of northern Kazakstan is a prolongation of the Western Siberian Plain and supports a predominantly Russian population in agriculture, mining and manu-facturing. Khrushchev's 'Virgin Lands Campaign' – intended to solve a chronic Soviet grain shortage without releasing the peasantry from the bonds of state and collective farming – pushed the frontier of arable cultivation too far into the semi-arid south, and much of the increment in sown area had to be abandoned in the face of inadequate precipitation and wind erosion. A second agricultural zone is along the approximately parallel courses of the Syr Darya and Amu Darya rivers, too little of whose waters reach the Aral Sea to reverse its disastrous dessication. Irrigation allows intensive growing of rice and cotton. More farmland, some of it very rich, is added in the basins of smaller rivers and oases, along the Kazak coast of the Caspian littoral (with the Emba and Ural rivers) and in the Uzbek part of the Fergana Valley. A third upland zone – rising in Kazakstan to the mountains of the Altai and Tien Shan, and in Uzbekistan surrounding the Fergana Valley – allows forestry and subalpine and alpine farming, but is economically important for mineral deposits. The fourth zone, covering a majority of the combined territory, is desert and semi-desert: its wealth is in oil, gas and coal, but in Soviet times its remoteness brought testing of nuclear and chemical weapons (respectively Semipalatinsk and Aral'sk), and the country's chief space station (Baikonur).

Habitat shaped the region's openness to penetration and to the direction of trading links. The only natural obstacles to population movement were mountain ranges to the east and southeast; the flat or rolling terrain which occupied the rest of the region invited migration and nomadism. The deserts inevitably remained empty, but settlements in the southern river zones can be dated back to the fourth millennium BC and in the northern plains from the second millennium BC; evidence of craftsmanship and irrigation in the south appears from the later half of the second millennium and nomadic pastoralists entered the northern areas early in the first millennium. By that time, the economic life of the region was roughly distributed between precipitation-based arable farming in the north, oasis and irrigated cultivation in the south, and stock-breeding nomads between them; arable, nomadic and transhumance were mixed in the eastern highlands. These divisions fashioned the organization of society. The city-based states in the south – Bactria, Khorezm and Sogdiana – were economically based on a tribute-paying intensive agriculture, their craftsmanship and eventually long-distance trade. The range and magnitude of commerce was greatly extended as the southern civilization fell under the sway of the Persian empire and later the Greeks under Alexander of Macedon (whose northernmost capture was Alexandria Eschata, the modern Khojent). Meanwhile tribal confederacies formed in the north, reflecting the shifting population and the sheer geographic space.

During the two millennia until about 1600 AD political dominion assured the southern cities economic access to the west, south and east. The Kashan empire from the Syr Darya (Jaxartes) and Amu Darya (Oxus) to the Indus basin lay between the Roman empire – which reached the Caspian at its furthest extent – and the Persian (Parthian and Sasanian) empires in the west and China in the east, and gained in power and wealth from the traffic on the Silk Road. Some Chinese influence was exerted in what is now eastern Kazakstan, but those parts remained nomadic. Turkic penetration in the sixth century (the Gök Türk empire) and conversion to Islam from the eighth century created the cultural entity which persists to this day, while the purchasing power of Byzantium and of China continued to assure profit from caravan trade and a peaceful development of farming and crafts. After the Arab conquest of Khorezm in 712, parts of what is now Uzbekistan became centres of high Arabic culture, epitomized by the polymaths Al-Biruni and Ibn Sina (Avicenna) at the turn of the eleventh century. The early Islamic centuries were marked both by the wealth

3

that could support art and science, and by a widening economic space: the Khorezmshahs were ruling from Anatolia to northern India on the eve of the Mongol invasion of 1219. The political unification of pastoral nomads, sedentary cultivators and trading cities under Gengiz Khan was, however, short-lived, for he divided his vast domain between his sons and the separation emerged of what was to become the Kazak and the Uzbek khanates. In the latter Amir Temur (Tamarlane) ruthlessly carved out an empire embracing all of Central Asia and Iran, as well as the Caucasus, Afghanistan and parts of India. He enriched his capital, Samarkand, and fostered production and trade as far afield as Europe, the Levant and China. Under his successors, his empire rapidly crumbled, to the benefit of neighbours, including the Kazaks. Competition among Kazak sultans for the fertile annexations around the Syr Darya and the town of Tashkent led to the formation of three distinct Hordes (from east to west, Big, Middle and Little), which formed 'relatively well-defined, independent tribe-states'.[2] At the same time the rulers of the mixed Uzbek and Tajik cities of Bukhara and Samarkand began to lose the commercial routes which they straddled: European shipping sailed around Africa to establish economic and political links with India and East Asia. The economy of the region was not pauperized, but stagnated as the traffic of the Silk Roads decayed.

The revival of long-distance trade came from the north. In the first half of the nineteenth century the Kazak Hordes fell to the Tsarist armies, which in the second half turned the remainder of Central Asia into colonies or protectorates. The interruption of cotton supply to Russian mills from the Confederate States during the American Civil War was a factor in the Tsarist annexation of a region already growing cheap cotton, but that crop, together with silk and minerals, assured a dominance for primary commodities; manufacturing – measured by employment in labour-intensive crafts – diminished under the impact of imported machine-made goods. Because the empire was a market economy, 'cottonization' was not pushed to the extremes of the Soviet period: in 1913 in Uzbekistan 70 per cent of the sown area was under grain and 19 per cent under cotton; by 1989 grain comprised 21 per cent and cotton 47 per cent.[3] As penetration increased by Russian and European commerce, the way to India was barred politically and the empires of Persia and China were economically unattractive. New trade routes flourished as the Russian railways drove down, but Central Asia was the end of the line.

Sovietization between 1918 and 1920 indicated new economic openings, postulated on corresponding anti-colonial change among 'Workers of the East'; the

[2] Shirin Akiner, *The Formation of Kazakh Identity: From Tribe to Nation-State*, FSS Key Paper, RIIA, London, 1995, ch. 3.
[3] Ünal Çeviköz, 'A Brief Account of the Economic Situation of the Former Soviet Republics of Central Asia,' *Central Asian Survey*, Vol. 13, No. 1, 1994, pp. 45–50.

'National Delimitation of Central Asia' in 1924–5 established, with only slight later changes, the frontiers of the five states as they are today.[4] From the end of the market-tolerant New Economic Policy until independence, Central Asia was economically subordinate to Stalin's dictum of 'Socialism in One Country' – to an autarkic command economy. The labour force was dragooned into Soviet institutions – collective farms and state enterprises – and its composition radically altered. More than a million fled the two republics between the Revolution and the early 1930s – Tajiks and Uzbeks after the defeat of the 'Kokand Autonomists' and the Basmachis, and Kazaks from forced collectivization and the settlement of nomads. Another million, mainly Kazaks, died in the coercion. In numbers they were replaced by immigrants, as a section below describes, most of whom were thrust into the post-1930 industrialization. Forced labourers developed the mining and metallurgy of Kazakstan;[5] technicians and professionals for industry in both republics were attracted by better food supply and housing than could be had in the Slav territories. More Slavs were imported into Kazak agriculture in the 1950s.

On the other hand, Moscow allowed only trickles of people and trade across international frontiers. Even when, in the late Soviet period, 'detente' and 'peaceful coexistence' became watchwords, and East–West trade expanded, this principally involved the Slavic Union Republics, Comecon and Western Europe. Under Brezhnev (1964–82) political events virtually sealed Central Asia's southern and eastern flanks – dispute with China, the Soviet invasion of Afghanistan and the Iranian Revolution. It is only since the USSR collapsed and the fifteen republics became independent in 1991 that Kazakstan and Uzbekistan have been able to undertake commerce with those states on economic grounds alone. In fact, both remain strongly dependent on the former Soviet market despite substantial trade promotion outside.

[4] Steven Sabol, 'The Creation of Soviet Central Asia: the 1924 National Delimitation', *Central Asian Survey*, Vol. 14, No. 2, 1995, pp. 225–41.
[5] The Aktyubinsk Chrome Combine, then the world's largest producer, had 17,347 prisoners at work in the last quarter of 1942 under GULGMP (Chief Administration of Camps of the Mining and Metallurgy Industry); the Dhzezkazgan Copper Combine at Karaganda had 11,443 prisoners on its roll (Edwin Bacon, *The Gulag at War: Stalin's Forced Labour System in the Light of the Archives*, London, Macmillan, 1994, pp. 74, 164–5). On the purchase of a majority share in the chrome industry by the Japan Chromium Corporation in 1996, see pp. 47–8.

Output and labour

In its *World Development Report 1996* the World Bank ranks 56 countries poorer than Kazakstan and Uzbekistan and 73 countries richer, all in terms of GNP per capita at established exchange rates.[6] At respectively $1,160 and $960 per capita, the Bank classes them as just within the 'lower middle-income' group, but (as Table 1 shows) recomputes the values to $2,810 and $2,370 at PPP. In such values, residents of each are better off than Azeris, Armenians, Georgians and Kyrgyz, but among the former Soviet republics they are poorer than the peoples of the Slav and Baltic republics. The divergence of the rich Union Republics getting richer and the poor getting poorer was a feature of the last two decades of Soviet power. By 1990 on the Soviet measure of national income, net material product (NMP is smaller than standard Western aggregates by the value of personal and public services), output per capita as a percentage of Russia's was 67 in Kazakstan and 38 in Uzbekistan, against respectively 82 and 61 in 1970. The relative decline – sharpest in the 1980s – was due to a faster decline in the efficiency with which capital assets were utilized (Kazakstan, Turkmenistan and Uzbekistan were worse than all other Soviet republics), slower labour productivity growth (Kazakstan, Tajikistan, Turkmenistan and Uzbekistan had the worst records) and a no more than average investment in new capital.[7] The origin of GDP altered significantly during the recessions. Between 1991 and 1995, as percentages of GDP at factor cost (i.e. excluding indirect taxes and subsidies), industrial output fell from 29 to 13 in Kazakstan and from 26 to 19 in Uzbekistan; agriculture held its share in Kazakstan (28 down to 27) but declined from 37 to 33 in Uzbekistan; the other branches (transport, communications, construction and services) correspondingly rose from 43 to 61 in Kazakstan and 38 to 48 in Uzbekistan.[8]

[6] World Bank, *From Plan to Market: World Development Report 1996*, Washington, DC, 1996, Table 1; the conversion to US dollars per capita is by its 'Atlas method', averaging exchange rates and inflation over three years, with 1994 the middle year, and population taken as that of mid-1994. On PPP see Table 1. The 'Technical Notes' to that Report and the revisions to those estimates (EBRD, *Transition Report 1996*, Annex 8.1) are only part of the many caveats in international and inter-temporal comparison. The new Statistical Offices of former Soviet republics are experiencing problems of data definition, collection and summation to economic and social indicators, and many statistics still need to be treated with caution.
[7] W. Easterly and S. Fischer, 'Growth Prospects for the Ex-Soviet Republics', in A. Aganbegyan, O. Bogomolov and M. Kaser (eds), *Economics in a Changing World*, Vol. 1: *System Transformation: Eastern and Western Assessments*, Macmillan, London, 1994, ch. 6.
[8] The Kazak series of GDP 1991–5 and Uzbek series 1991–3 are on the database of the UN Economic Commission for Europe (access to which is appreciatively acknowledged); the Uzbek data for 1995 are from the IMF Country Study (96/73, Table 3), deducting the 'net tax sector' from gross value added.

During Soviet industrialization, the one resource which all Central Asian republics were able to capture for economic growth was labour, but the excess from rural areas and from historically large families permitted even greater overemployment than in the rest of the USSR, with the poor productivity record just shown. Uzbekistan differs from Kazakstan in still having much disguised unemployment in agriculture and in maintaining a high demographic growth. The smallest estimate of underemployment in Uzbekistan is one million out of an economically active 8.9 million, and the largest is that four million are either nominally or partially employed. With an annual excess of births over deaths per 1,000 population of 27.6 per cent in 1990 and 22.7 per cent in 1994, there will be an increment of nearly one million in the working-age population by the year 2000. There is rural underemployment also in southern Kazakstan, and temporary redundancy and labour-force withdrawal elsewhere in the republic. But natural population growth fell from 21.7 to 16.6 per cent between 1990 and 1995, and fell even faster among Russian households.[9]

The post-independence fall in output (faster in NMP than in GNP because the service sector expanded) has not been accompanied by the large 'labour shake-out' that market economies experience with recession; in common with most former Soviet republics, state enterprises have been forced to curtail production but have retained most of their workforce. In mid-1994, 250,000 workers in Uzbekistan were being paid 70 per cent of their average wage but were not required to work (this was termed 'administrative leave'); the government subsidizes such payments, which are regarded as socially more acceptable than unemployment benefit. Those on so-called 'forced leave' (without any pay) in late 1995 numbered 183,000 in Kazakstan and 60,000 in Uzbekistan; those on unemployment benefit were then 74,000 in Kazakstan and 31,000 in Uzbekistan.[10] Privatization diminished the number of firms which could claim such subsidy, while creating vacancies which have absorbed some of those without work. Privatized firms are, however, rarely taking over the social and health-care facilities available to those employed or on 'leave'. Both governments' policies of monetary stabilization have reduced the funds available for workplace subsidy, and for health-care, education and other social provision; the effects of such drastic cuts – and the virtual elimination of capital expenditure in this sector – are discussed below.

[9] These and much other data in this study are from *Kratky statistichesky ezhegodnik Kazakhstana 1995*, State Committee for Statistics, Almaty, 1996, *Basic Results of Social and Economic Development of the Republic of Uzbekistan, January–June 1996*, State Committee for Forecasting and Statistics, Tashkent, 1996, and IMF Staff Country Reports: No. 96/22, *Kazakstan – Recent Economic Developments*, March 1996, and No. 96/73, *Uzbekistan – Selected Issues and Statistical Appendix*, August 1996. Population data are also from UN Development Programme, *Kazakstan Human Development Report 1996*, UNDP, Almaty, 1996.

[10] The IMF cites unemployment on the ILO definition, but for Uzbekistan *Basic Results*, pp. 80, 88, show 0.6 per cent reportedly on that definition.

Spending on unemployment benefit has been kept below that appropriate to the numbers actually made redundant. Registered unemployment in mid-1995 was 1.9 per cent in Kazakstan and 0.4 per cent in Uzbekistan; on the ILO definition of unemployment, it was likely to have been 6 per cent in the former and 2.2 per cent in the latter. Since then the labour situation in Kazakstan has deteriorated: on 1 June 1996, recorded unemployment was reported as 3.6 per cent, to which should be added 5.5 per cent hidden unemployment (four out of five of whom were without pay).[11] In both states total employment had been stable until 1993, but then declined – from 5,625,000 in 1993 to 4,498,000 in 1995 in Kazakstan and from 8,259,000 in 1993 to 8,158,000 in 1995 in Uzbekistan.[12] Reasons for the greater decline in employment in Kazakstan than in Uzbekistan included more emigration and a steeper decline in non-farm economic activity.

Uzbekistan, in fact, suffered least among the former Soviet states from post-independence recession. Table 1 shows that GDP in 1996 was likely to be 82 per cent of that of 1989, whereas in Kazakstan it was 46 per cent; the range in the other states of the CIS ranged from 20 per cent in Georgia through 53 in Russia to 60 per cent in Turkmenistan. The principal causes of the post-Soviet decline are the familiar three factors: first, the centralized supply system of Soviet planning disappeared and enterprises throughout the former Soviet Union had to establish individual contracts where prices and deliveries had previously been dictated; secondly, the abolition of the Council for Mutual Economic Assistance (CMEA) meant that deliveries to and from such partners were no longer embodied in government-to-government protocols, and enterprises sought to switch trade to the West; and, thirdly, demand fell for a large number of goods – military orders (such as for the important defence and space facilities in Kazakstan and for the Uzbek aircraft industry) were cut and consumer-goods producers were hit by foreign imports when currency and trade controls were relaxed. That the decline was smaller in Uzbekistan than elsewhere in the former Soviet Union is due to a number of factors. First, Uzbekistan had, as noted, a high share of agriculture, which was less vulnerable to the trade shock, and a relatively low share of defence industry, affected by the deep defence cuts. Secondly, its terms of trade improved as the prices of gold and cotton rose, and export deliveries persisted within the CIS despite non-payment of invoices by recipients. Thirdly, the government supported enterprises which faced slacker or even

---

[11] *Central Asia Newsfile* (School of Oriental and African Studies, London University), June 1996, p. 4.
[12] With one exception, these figures are from the IMF Staff Country Reports, but Kazak employment in 1995 is from *Kazakstan Economic Trends*, First Quarter 1996, Table 4.1 (prepared for the Government of Kazakstan by the European Expertise Service of the European Commission, TACIS Programme), in which the series differs from the IMF record and *Kratky statistichesky ezhegodnik*, p. 21. From January 1996 the IMF series is discontinuous, owing to the inclusion of more than half a million workers on collective farms.

zero demand.[13] These same factors were especially deleterious for Kazakstan. Budget expenditure on the 'national economy', which is principally subsidies and maintenance outlays, was cut from 6 per cent of GDP in 1993 to 3.7 per cent in 1995, but substantial payments arrears remained (of the order of 2 per cent of GDP). To these must be added heavy inter-enterprise arrears, which on a gross basis rose from 86 billion tenge debts receivable in January 1995 to 230 billion in December (net of debts repayable, from 37 to 127 billion).[14] Kazenergo has cut power supply to whole regions in which it has debtors for electricity, but in turn has been shorn of input by its Russian grid partner; Russia claimed a total of $500 million in debts, though the Kazak government claims this was $370 million because Russia had arrears on coal purchases and rent for the Baikonur space centre.[15]

To list reasons why the Uzbek GDP declined so little until 1995 and why the Kazak GDP fell so sharply is also to indicate why one could justifiably anticipate for 1996 a further Uzbek decline and a Kazak upturn. This in fact happened. The Uzbek programme agreed for that year with the IMF envisaged a 1.5 per cent fall, against an actual 1.2 per cent decline in 1995: the outcome is likely to be a 1 per cent decline. The weightiest consideration was the pressure by the IMF and other external institutions to reduce the government's expenditure, notably in support of subsidized industry, farming and social services, so that there was a closer balance with revenue; the 1996 budget deficit was planned at 4 per cent of GDP (which proved to be that of 1995), against 18 per cent of a larger GDP back in 1992. Another reason is that enterprise restructuring, much of it after privatization or sale to foreigners, brought labour redundancies – and hence reduced household purchasing power – which only slowly found employment in the resurgent private sector. In 1992 the current-account deficit had been 11.8 per cent of GDP and was still 9 per cent in 1993.[16] Exports revived sufficiently in 1994 to show a current-account surplus but they shrank disastrously in 1995 when (as prospectively in 1996)[17] the country ran a deficit, despite a decimation (literally to one-tenth of the 1994 level) of energy imports and a one-third cut in purchases of food and other agricultural produce (as

---

[13] See Akhad Agzamov, Alisher Anvarov and Kahramon Shakirov, 'Economic Reform and Investment Priorities in the Republic of Uzbekistan', *Comparative Economic Studies*, Vol. 37, No. 3, Fall 1995, pp. 27–38.

[14] *Kazakstan Economic Trends*, May 1996, Table 11.2.

[15] *Financial Times*, 3 October 1996; a Russo-Kazak agreement of March 1994 declared the space station to be owned by Kazakhstan, but rented for 20 years at $115 million annually (Shireen T. Hunter, *Central Asia since Independence*, Praeger, Westport CT, 1996, p. 121).

[16] IMF Staff Country Report No. 95/23, *Republic of Uzbekistan: Background Paper and Statistical Appendix*, March 1995, Table 7.

[17] EBRD, *Transition Report 1996*, gives $53 million as the 1995 current account deficit and projects $512 million for 1996, against an earlier official forecast of $620 million.

part of a drive to grain self-sufficiency). The seriousness of the external position was attenuated by bullion sales – because independent Uzbekistan inherited two major gold-mining complexes – but competitive exports and foreign capital inflow (which are of course related because foreign implants generate marketable products) are crucial to its future, as they are to Kazakstan's.

That upturn is feasible is borne out by the experience of Kazakstan and of central and eastern Europe and the Baltic states: transition economies are recovering in the medium term. The latter group of 13 countries exhibited a 4 per cent GDP gain in 1996, attaining 90 per cent of their 1989 level. The eastern *Länder* of Germany (the former GDR) and Poland have regained their 1989 levels in aggregate, but in very different composition. Kazakstan, which had a 9 per cent GDP decline in 1995, achieved a 1 per cent GDP increment in the first half of 1996, its first since independence, and probably 0.5 per cent over the full year. One factor was consumer and investor confidence as inflation was checked – the consumer price index at a monthly rate was as low as 1.9 per cent in March 1996, and real wages had risen 9 per cent in 1995.

Human development

Output and labour indicators show Kazakstan and Uzbekistan as typical less-developed countries, with surplus labour, low capital and labour productivity, modest GDP per capita, a large farm sector slowly adjusting to agrarian reform, and minerals ripe for exploitation. A more perceptive comparison with the typical Third World economy demonstrates, however, the results of significant human development over the past sixty years.[18] In the first place, the labour force is much better educated than in similar developing economies, and has a highly-skilled core. Literacy is almost universal (97.5 per cent in Kazakstan and 97.2 per cent in Uzbekistan[19] – many bilingually), and almost all children of the relevant age are enrolled in secondary education – in Kazakstan 89 per cent of males and 91 per cent of females and in Uzbekistan 96 per cent of males and 92 per cent of females.[20] For

---

[18] The focus on a combination of social and economic measures and objectives in 'human development' owes much in the present context to the UNDP – see *Kazakstan Human Development Report 1996*; to Keith Griffin (ed.), *Social Policy and Economic Transformation in Uzbekistan*, ILO and UNDP, Geneva, 1996; and to the assistance arm of the European Commission – see Greg Kaser (Project Director), *Social Policy and Enterprise Restructuring in Kazakstan*, TACIS, 3 vols, Brussels, 1996 (hereafter TACIS Report).

[19] Igor Kitaev (ed.), *Educational Finance in Central Asia and Mongolia*, UNESCO: IIEP, Paris, 1996, p. 72.

[20] 1993 data from *World Development Report 1996*, Table 7. The UNDP's *Kazakstan Human Development Report*, Box 3.3.1, points out that in rural areas only 52 per cent of secondary schools retain children until age 17, whereas 78 per cent do so in urban areas.

comparison, a secular Muslim state such as Egypt, at about the same income level, has for males 61 per cent literacy and 79 per cent in secondary school, and for females 36 per cent literacy and 81 per cent in secondary school. Because education as an investment yields production until retirement age, it is relevant that the expectation of life at birth in 1994 was 68 years in Kazakstan and 70 years in Uzbekistan, bettered in the CIS only by Belarusians and the traditionally long-lived Caucasians. Because each government has made the maintenance of social protection its economic anchor, life expectancy at birth has since independence been constant in Kazakstan and has risen in Uzbekistan: within the CIS only Georgia and Turkmenistan have also shown an increase. Although the availability of health-care facilities has shrunk and morbidity from a number of diseases has risen, the commonly accepted index of general health, infant mortality, has, at least as yet, been unaffected: it has been almost constant in Kazakstan (26.4 per thousand live births in 1990, rising to 28.4 in 1993, but down to 27.7 in 1995) and has fallen in Uzbekistan (34.6 in 1990, 25.7 in 1994).[21] Health experience, however, is regionally differentiated. As a percentage of causes of death, circulatory disease was high in Taldykorgan *oblast* (56) but low in Atyrau (32), whereas cancer was high in Northern Kazakstan *oblast* (18) but low in Taldykorgan *oblast*. The latter stands out as having the lowest alcohol consumption – 0.74 litres of pure alcohol annually (1994) – as befits a region of Islamic tradition, whereas in the colder, Slav-inhabited areas of the north and east the quantities are respectively 2.93 and 4.59 litres; these are also among the regions seriously affected by atmospheric pollution.[22]

Education was the last public sector to be hit by the reduction of budget spending in the interest of fiscal balance: it absorbed almost the same share of gross domestic expenditure in Kazakstan in 1995 as in 1992 (3.1 against 3.5 per cent), although the share declined in Uzbekistan (from 10.1 to 7.5 per cent) – partly because the local contribution to education spending has regularly been higher in Kazakstan that in Uzbekistan.[23] In the latter, the education authorities, by eliminating virtually all capital expenditure (only 4 per cent in 1994 against 16 per cent in 1985), maintained current spending on schools and higher education. In the longer

---

[21] The complex of issues underlying the demographic experiences of transition are examined in Giovanni Andrea Cornia and Renato Paniccia (eds), *Demographic Impact of Sudden Impoverishment: Eastern Europe during the 1989–94 Transition*, UNICEF, Florence, 1995; Michael Kaser and Santosh Mehrotra, 'The Central Asian Economies after Independence', in Roy Allison (ed.), *Challenges for the Former Soviet South*, RIIA/Brookings Institution, Washington DC, 1996, pp. 287–9. These and other relevant data are in the latter, IMF Staff Country Reports, and *Kazakstan Human Development Report 1996*.

[22] All data for 1994 (*Kazakstan Human Development Report*, pp. 99–101).

[23] Kitaev, *Educational Finance*, pp. 14 and 73 (which shows a developed economy average in 1990 of 5.2 per cent of GNP); IMF Staff Country Reports, 96/22 and 96/73.

term the effects will be felt of a serious loss of teachers (who, paid relatively worse than the average worker, are leaving for private-sector enterprise) and the deterioration of physical facilities.[24] Primary and secondary education in Kazakstan and pre-school education in Uzbekistan were particularly protected, in response to demographic pressure. It is perhaps because a sound educational and health base been achieved that some social surveys show provision in those sectors as the least of popular concerns. For example in Aktyubinsk (Kazakstan) the ranking of public worries in early 1996 put inflation at the top, followed by real income decline, uncertainty of obtaining housing, unemployment and the loss of job security, but the reduced availability of free or subsidized services (health care and utilities) and of education at the bottom.[25]

Between 1965 and 1990 the proportion of specialists with higher education in the population had risen sixfold in Kazakstan and tripled in Uzbekistan, and in principle such specialists should be available for work in technologically advanced industries and especially enterprises being implanted from abroad. There is evidence, however, that many have been driven out of scientific and technical employment by the reduction of government funding for research and development and by the loss of the drive for technological parity with NATO weaponry – the USSR devoted more of its research and development to defence than the NATO powers. On the basis of the 'East German scenario' of the displacement of R&D staff out of specialist employment, a member of the Sussex University Science Policy Research Unit has shown that all transition countries have gone through a corresponding phase and that Kazakstan and Uzbekistan appear among the worst affected.[26]

Emigration to Russia

Another reason for the decline in R&D employment is the heavy emigration – beginning in the first half of the 1970s in Kazakstan and the second half in Uzbekistan[27] – of Slav settlers from these and the other Central Asian states. At the first postwar census (1959) in Kazakstan there were one-and-a-half times as many Russians as Kazaks; the total Slav population was nearly five million. Only a handful of them declared Kazak to be their mother tongue, but 8 per cent of Kazaks declared Russian. At the

[24] Igor Kitaev (ed.), *Assessment of Training Needs in Educational Planning and Management (with Special Reference to Central Asia)*, UNESCO/IIEP, Paris, 1995, p. 26.
[25] Greg Kaser, *TACIS Report*, Vol. 1, p. 20.
[26] Slavo Radosevic, 'Science and Technology Capabilities in Economies in Transition: Effects and Prospects,' *Economics of Transition*, Vol. 3, No. 4, 1995, pp. 459–78.
[27] Tabulation by quinquennia and detailed commentary in Anatoli Vishnevski, 'L'Asie centrale post-soviétique: reflet du passé et miroir des changements en cours', *Revue d'études comparatives Est-Ouest*, Vol. 26, No. 4, pp. 101–23.

1970 census Slavs were still a majority (51.1 per cent) but they were in a minority by the 1979 census. Uzbeks at the 1959 census outnumbered Russians (13.5 per cent of the population) five to one, but there were nevertheless 1.2 million Slavs. By 1993, however, Russians numbered only 35 per cent of the population of Kazakstan (38 per cent in 1989) and 7 per cent of Uzbekistan (8 per cent in 1989). Between 1990 and 1994, 483,000 migrants entered Russia from Kazakstan (8 per cent of the Russian residents of 1989) and 278,000 from Uzbekistan (17 per cent of 1989 Russians).[28] The disallowance of dual nationality (accorded in Kyrgyzstan and Turkmenistan and awaiting only ratification by the Russian Duma for Tajikistan) has affected the decisions of Slav residents to leave, despite political stability and a government policy of ethnic tolerance. The number might have been larger but for the prospect of unemployment due to the persistent recession in Belarus, Russia and Ukraine, higher living costs and longer-term considerations such as a more rigorous climate and a lack of local and family ties for returnees.[29] Many German households, usually of high skills, deported from the Volga region during the Second World War, have left for Germany.

Some emigration is offset by the return of ethnic households from the Slav republics, hit by unemployment, discrimination (the Chechen problem has brought some disparagement of any 'southerner' in Russia) and the attraction of responsible posts in their home republic. The centralized bureaucracy of Party and government brought many from the 'periphery' to Moscow where their children had an elite education and corresponding opportunities, including stays abroad for study or work. This new generation, although numerically small, is having some effect on the stock of expertise; on balance, however, these people may be less skilled than the emigrants they replace. More effective is the increasing staff of foreign firms being established in the two republics and the specialists and advisers on missions of the international agencies and bilateral assistance programmes. Other incomers are Uighurs from Xinjiang in the Chinese People's Republic – there are now at least 200,000 in Kazakstan[30] – and those displaced by hostilities in Afghanistan and

[28] For these data and a commentary see Christina Codagnone in Helma Lutz and Khalid Koser (eds), *New Migration in Europe: Social Constructions and Social Realities,* Macmillan, London, forthcoming. Yalman Onaran, 'Economics and Nationalism: The Case of Muslim Central Asia', *Central Asian Survey,* Vol. 13, No. 4, 1994, pp. 491–505, in a concise history of migrant-autochthonous relations, notes under-employment in the 1970s and 1980s as fostering 'anti-foreigner' sentiments among the local nationalities.

[29] A survey of reasons given by Russians for departure from Central Asia is in Catherine Poujol, 'Minorités exogènes ou Russes de l'intérieur en Asie centrale,' *Revue d'études comparatives Est-Ouest,* Vol. 26, No. 4, pp. 125–42.

[30] *Financial Times,* 25 May 1996, which also discusses the Sino-Kazak political problems Uighur migrants generate. Among accounts of the secessionist Uighur movements across the Sino-Kazak frontier, see Christa Paula, *The Road to Miran. Travels in the Forbidden Zone of Xinjiang,* HarperCollins-Flamingo, London, 1995, pp. 267–70; continuance of the unrest is documented in *Central Asia Newsfile,* June 1996, p. 2.

Tajikistan. Problems persist with the Uzbek minority in Tajikistan and the Tajik minority in Uzbekistan (registered as 5 per cent, but possibly between 25 and 30 per cent[31]).

A sample survey in Tashkent in 1994 showed that of respondents 60 per cent of Russians had graduated from tertiary education, but only 44 per cent of Uzbeks; as a rough measure of professional standing, 41 per cent of Russians, but only 4 per cent of Uzbeks, had a monthly income above 800 sum.[32] Such haemorrhage of trained personnel as has occurred has affected chiefly the civil service, banking, medicine, industrial management and technology, and the replacement of emigrants is patently important for the enhancement of productivity, in which, as already indicated, performance has hitherto been poor. More than a hundred technical and higher education institutions are locally available for such training, and research and development is undertaken in a further hundred scientific institutes. The space research centre at Baikonur in Kazakstan and the International Centre for High-Temperature Solar Physics and the Astrophysics Centre in Uzbekistan may be singled out, together with the Uzbekistan Institute for Bio-organic Chemistry, which has generated new natural dyes and biological methods of plant protection.

Urban–rural distribution

Both governments encourage small and medium-sized businesses in rural areas, in order to employ the available workforce locally in labour-intensive activity and to discourage further urbanization – Tashkent already has more than 2.1 million residents and Almaty 1.2 million. In Kazakstan twenty towns, and in Uzbekistan fifteen, have over 100,000. The transfer of the Kazak capital to Akmola (formerly Tselinograd or Akmolinsk), currently with a population of 300,000, is intended both to locate into the more industrialized northeast and to check the growth of Almaty. A UNDP report points out that rural employment in Uzbekistan has increased since independence, while farm output has shrunk.[33] Neither republic needs more labour in agriculture, but non-farm development in rural areas and small towns can reduce the need for new housing, the construction of which costs more per person in cities and in the earthquake-prone regions (Almaty and Tashkent included). Similarly, enterprises with low capital-to-labour and capital-to-output ratios require less start-

[31] The upper estimates are from Richard Foltz, 'The Tajiks of Uzbekistan', *Central Asian Survey*, Vol. 15, No. 2, 1996, pp. 213–6. But Annette Bohr, unpublished paper, forthcoming in the RIIA's Former Soviet South series, puts 15 per cent as an upper bound.
[32] Craig Smith, 'An Economic Analysis of Ethnicity in Uzbekistan', *Comparative Economic Studies*, Vol. 37, No. 2, Summer 1995, pp. 97–110.
[33] Keith Griffin (ed.), *Social Policy*, p. 41.

up capital, enlarge the private sector, and enhance the quality of farm produce (packing, packaging, transport and trading). The policy adding value to farm produce is paralleled by encouragement for more diverse and higher-quality crops and livestock and the broad objective of substituting domestic for imported foodstuffs.

A report to the TACIS service of the European Commission (led by International Economic and Energy Consultants of the UK) recommends four measures with which the Kazakstan authorities could stimulate small and medium-sized enterprises. First, procedures for registering new businesses could be simplified and concentrated in a single district office, with the service widely advertised. Secondly, local taxes could be waived for, say, the first two years of operation. Thirdly, official assistance could be offered for small initial investments, provided that the evaluation of requests was transparently conducted. Finally, training in entrepreneurship should begin at an early age in schools and further education.[34] Such recommendations would apply also to Uzbekistan, which has vigorously promoted the third through a state-owned commercial bank, Pakhta Bank, established in July 1995 to furnish credit for these and farm enterprises. The weak banking system of Kazakstan is serviced in this sector by the Soviet-period Agroprombank, which is burdened by non-performing loans.[35]

Enhancing value-added in rural areas would reduce the spread of income distribution. In both states, but more in Uzbekistan, income per household member has been lower in rural areas than in urban, mainly because of larger family size and smaller household revenue. More broadly, the spread of personal income distribution has widened. In Kazakstan in 1989 the revenue share of the poorest two-fifths of the population was 23 per cent of all personal revenues; in 1994 it was only 19 per cent. The upper one-fifth had the same share – 34 per cent in both years – and the middle class were the gainers. A sample of 6,000 households in August 1995 showed 84 per cent of the rural, and 44 per cent of the urban, population below the poverty line.[36] Dispersion of personal incomes has also become greater in Uzbekistan: the average of the richest tenth of the population was 3.5 times that of the poorest tenth in 1991, but 8.7 times in 1993.[37] Fiscal pressures are modifying both governments' policies to maintain the existing social safety net and their reliance on the trickle-down effect of general economic growth must be long- rather than short-term. Targeting the most vulnerable groups is not easy. In Uzbekistan, under a 1995 programme of social allowances, the take-up was minimal among the

---

[34] Greg Kaser, *TACIS Report*, Vol. 1, p. 14.
[35] IMF Staff Country Report 96/22, p. 39; the Bank was recapitalized in February 1996 and sale of some of its state equity envisaged (*Kazakstan Economic Trends*, First Quarter 1996, p. 42).
[36] *Kazakstan Human Development Report 1996*, pp. 52–3.
[37] Kaser and Mehrotra, in Allison (ed.), *Challenges...*, p. 264.

376,000 women eligible for a special benefit as mothers of children under two years of age.[38] This may possibly have been due to a reluctance to claim separately from their partners. To combat this, the Uzbek government now pays a new 'material assistance to low-income families' to a local community body (*mahalla*) to distribute as it perceives the need. The *mahalla* system also provides a focus for social cohesion as collective and state farms are disbanded.

The export base of natural resources

Among the Central Asian states Kazakstan and Uzbekistan have the most diversified and substantial export potential in economically usable mineral resources; some of the latter's deposits overlap with those of Turkmenistan, the wealth of which is heavily linked to hydrocarbons. A list of such resources includes in both republics the three principal energy carriers – gas, oil and coal, in that order – as exportables. Among metals both have copper, lead, molybdenum, tungsten, uranium and zinc, with beryllium, chromite, iron ore, manganese, tantalum and titanium in Kazakstan.[39] Both states have large resources of building materials (particularly cement, gypsum, marble and other facing stone in both, with refractory clays also in Kazakstan); alunite, asbestos, barite, bauxite, bismuth, castorite, corundum, fluorspar, graphite, iodine-bromine, kaolin, ozocerite, quartz, soda and sulphur; plus chemicals for fertilizer (nitrates and phosphates). Copper output, running annually at around 260,000 tonnes in Kazakstan and 80,000 tonnes in Uzbekistan, is internationally competitive, and Kazakstan's share of world output is also significant (normally exceeding 5 per cent) in barite, beryllium, chromite, lead, manganese, silver, tantalum, titanium, tungsten, uranium and zinc. Kazakstan has small but promising diamond pipes and a rich array of semi-precious stones. The exploitation of precious metals is long-established in Kazakstan, but recent in Uzbekistan. Although gold ores were mined in the Angren River basin (Uzbekistan) between 800 and 1,100 years ago, the region's modern industry dates from the opening of the Ridder mine in the Kazak Altai in 1794. The Ridder-Sokol'noe and Tishinskoe mines, united in the Leninogorsk Polymetallic Combine, have been Kazakstan's principal non-ferrous and gold suppliers, but now possess only ten years' reserves; further sources of copper, lead, zinc, silver and gold are being developed in the same zone. In addition to by-product gold (at many other sites), Kazakstan has two major gold mines, Bakyrchik and

---

[38] IMF, Staff Country Report 96/73, pp. 26–7.

[39] A list of mineral deposits, the availability of geological maps and a statement of policy of Serikbek Daukeyev, Minister of Geology and Underground Resources, is in *Mineral Resources of Kazakstan* (bilingual version of *Mineral'nye resursy Kazakhstana*), September 1995.

16

Vasilovskoe; problems arising from these two foreign joint ventures are discussed in Chapter 3 (pp. 46–7). Production in 1994 was 14 tonnes, but reserves are still a state secret. Uzbekistan began substantial gold extraction only when an important lode was revealed at Muruntau in the Kyzyl Kum Desert in 1958; deposits in the Angren region had already been reopened and more major lodes (notably Mardzhanbulak) were exploited in the ensuing decade. Joint ventures are in operation there as well and are also discussed in Chapter 3 (p. 46). In all, Uzbekistan has more than 4,000 tonnes of gold deposits, and its production, at 70 tonnes in 1995, is in the world's top ten.

During peak production years, both republics were among the world's leading exporters of uranium. Kazak output has declined (to a low of 3,000 tonnes in 1992), but is reviving in a joint venture of Katep with two Canadian uranium producers. Uzbekistan has a large potential, with more than 400 deposits containing an estimated 230,000 tonnes. The international concern aroused by the storage of radioactive waste from Kyrgyz uranium mines may indicate corresponding problems. Overall, of 1995 output of mining and manufacturing in Kazakstan, 28 per cent derived from minerals extraction, 23 per cent from fossil fuels, 4 per cent from ferrous metallurgy and 12 per cent from non-ferrous metallurgy.[40]

Kazakstan's steel production is based on its own ore (running at 25 million tonnes a year in 1980–90, but only 15 million tonnes in 1995) and Karaganda coal (from 131 million tonnes in 1990 to 83 million in 1995), which produced 4 million tonnes of metallurgical coke at the end of the Soviet period, but less than 2 million tonnes by 1994–5. The Karmet steel plant at Karaganda is one of the world's largest steel mills and the coking coal deposits are among the world's biggest, exceeding one billion tonnes. The whole combine, apart from opencast coal, has been taken over by a London-based private company, Ispat, which, with $200 million capital promised and a restructuring and redundancy plan, anticipates long-run cost-effective production. By contrast, Uzbekistan has small iron ore deposits (at most 60 million tonnes), but this did not inhibit the building of a steel works near Bekabad in the Fergana Valley in 1944 as part of the eastward evacuation of heavy industry during the Second World War. Output expanded during the 1980s to a million tonnes of steel and of rolled products. Bekabad (producing 550,000 tonnes in 1995) is being completely rebuilt, with German and Russian components, for completion in 1998. Even at half-capacity for steel and producing only 300,000 tonnes of rolled metal, it required imports amounting to 11.9 per cent of the 1995 CIS import bill, but earned a mere 1.6 per cent of CIS exports.

[40] *Promyshlennost' Respubliki Kazakhstana (statistichesky spravochnik)*, Almaty, 1996, p. 9.

On the eve of substantial hydrocarbon exports by each state, both states are net energy exporters – Kazakstan coal and oil sales exceed electricity and gas purchases, while Uzbekistan's gas and electricity sales (and the balance on its trivial trade in coal) exceed oil imports. Gas from Gazli and associated deposits, near Bukhara, has been a staple Uzbek export for three decades: the pipeline to Russian consumers, completed in 1963, was then the world's longest at 4,503 km; the second, of 1967, was the world's widest at 1,220 mm. Gazli, however, is approaching exhaustion – in 1995 the fall in gas output from these deposits was offset by a 15 per cent rise in oil and a 6 per cent rise in condensate – and will be soon replaced by output from the Shurtan and Zevardy fields. The extraction of natural gas at Mubarek also provides elemental sulphur. Overall, gas in Uzbekistan remains very important as a domestic fuel (over 70 per cent of electricity generation is gas-fired, the remainder being hydropower) and for export: hydrocarbons earned $333 million in 1995, but all went to the CIS, Kyrgyzstan taking exactly half of it. Uzbekistan alone among CIS states in the first four years of independence increased its oil and gas extraction – to 47.2 billion cu. m of gas and 5.5 million tonnes of oil in 1994. In 1995, whereas oil showed a substantial further rise to 7.9 million tonnes, the decline of Gazli led to an overall fall of gas to 40.8 million cu. m. The official forecast for gas in the year 2000 is 60 billion cu. m – from proven and probable reserves assessed at end-1994 as 1,848 billion cu. m, with 2,405 billion cu. m as estimated undiscovered deposits. Oil reserves are estimated as 244 million tonnes. Electricity generation (54.2 million MWh in 1991, and 47.7 million MWh in 1994) fell because the recession reduced demand and has not recovered because water flow was low in 1995.

Prospects of energy sales to Europe from Kazakstan are indubitably promising in oil and gas, but exports of coal depend on CIS markets. Deposits are estimated as 4.5 billion tonnes of oil, 1.6 billion tonnes of gas condensate and 5.9 trillion cu. m of gas.[41] The present 160 prospected deposits are in two districts: the richest, including the Tengiz field, around and under the Caspian Sea in northwestern Kazakstan; and in the central Aryskum trough. Gas is also in northwestern and in western Kazakstan and in the central regions in the Chu-Sarysu Basin. The northwestern hydrocarbons are being exploited with foreign investment (see Chapter 3).

[41] Confederation of British Industry (CBI), *Doing Business in Kazakstan*, Kogan Page, London, 1995, p. 62 (chapter contributed by the firm Ernst and Young). Lower (beginning of 1993) estimates are given by A. N. Poginov, 'Problems and Prospects of the Oil and Gas Complex of the Republic of Kazakhstan' in E. M. Kozhokin (ed.), *Kazakhstan: realii i perspektivy nezavisimogo razvitiya*, Russian Institute for Strategic Studies, Moscow, 1995, pp. 73–89. The latter provides a detailed survey of the exploitation of the individual deposits.

Farming and fisheries

The principal export crops are grain (mainly wheat), wool and meat from Kazakstan and cotton from Uzbekistan. In the perestroika period, Kazakstan supplied 27 per cent of Soviet wheat, 23 per cent of wool and 7 per cent of meat, and Uzbekistan 62 per cent of cotton. As noted above, both republics import foodstuffs from elsewhere in the CIS.[42] The staple exports of each have been subject to wide fluctuations. Thus Kazak grain production was 32 million tonnes in 1992 (permitting 22 million tonnes to be sold to Russia), but only half that in 1994 and under 10 million tonnes in 1995; the Uzbek cotton crop by 1995 had regained the 1992 level (both 4.1 million tonnes in raw fibre terms), but, though better than the 3.9 million tonnes of 1994, was well below that of the Soviet period (5.1 million tonnes in 1986–9) and a very poor 3.3 million tonnes was expected for 1996. The Soviet overemphasis on extensive grain in Kazakstan and on intensive cotton in Uzbekistan was disastrous to the natural environment. Part of north-central Kazakstan was transformed into a dust-bowl under the Virgin Lands Campaign in the decade from 1954. In Uzbekistan the manner of irrigation and heavy application of fertilizer and pesticide brought salination, water pollution and the drying of the Aral Sea. Present policy, supported by a $66 million World Bank credit granted in July 1995, is towards environmentally better farming on a smaller area frees the land to regain the grain self-sufficiency of the 1920s. The Uzbek grain harvest – 2.1 and 1.5 million tonnes in 1988 and 1989 – achieved 2.7 million tonnes in 1995; the Agriculture Ministry's target for 1996 was ambitious at 5 million tonnes.

The shrinkage of the Aral Sea has catastrophically reduced the local Kazak, Uzbek and Turkmen fisheries, but freshwater catches are still accessible in Kazakstan's many lakes. The most valuable seafood was caviar, from sturgeon in the lower Ural River and the adjoining Caspian waters.[43] The collapse of Soviet fishery regulation and hatcheries has quickly led to overfishing, which is destroying female fish before they are mature enough to produce the eggs; 90 per cent of caviar from Russian waters reportedly comes from poaching.[44] The joint efforts now being made to salvage the situation may already be too late.

[42] Igor Lipovski, 'The Central Asian Cotton Epic', *Central Asian Survey*, Vol. 14, No. 4, 1995, pp. 529–42, concludes that 'cottonization' induced 'the acute shortage of food crops in the region'.
[43] The Atyrau *oblast* Office of Internal Affairs reported in spring 1996 that in six months on the Ural River 600 poachers had been arrested and 20 tonnes of sturgeon, with 500 kg of caviar, confiscated (*Central Asia Newsfile*, June 1996, p. 10).
[44] *The Times*, 13 November 1996.

Environmental damage

Water pollution and wastage, overfishing and uranium disposal are far from the only damage inflicted on the environment and ecology of the two republics in the Soviet period. Some deleterious effects were unconnected with natural resource exploitation, such as the testing of nuclear weapons in the Semipalatinsk 'polygon'[45] and of chemical warfare technology at Aral'sk, but most relate to the lack of adequate filtration or protective work at mining and manufacturing installations. Many such were built and operated by forced labour from the 1930s to the 1950s, supplemented after 1941 by prisoners of war and deported populations. Within these republics, the latter included Volga Germans, Chechens, Ingush, Crimean Tatars and Koreans.[46] Because their lives and health were held in scant regard by their custodians, even less attention and money was devoted to human welfare than was the norm in Soviet 'production first' planning and practice. The noxious effects of the heavy and persistent emission of particulates and other harmful substances by metallurgy in Karaganda, Balkhash and Tursunzode (the latter in Tajikistan, but affecting adjoining districts of southern Uzbekistan) is now well documented. The problem is by its nature localized: thus sulphur and nitrogen emissions in 1993 in Kazakstan *oblasts* ranged from 4 kg in Almaty to 483 kg in Pavlodar and 957 kg in Jezkazgan.[47] The population of the Aral Sea basin has been affected by a combination of the desiccation of the sea, the release of salt, dust and sand into the food chain and water pollution from the inflow of herbicides, fertilizer and pesticides; the Caspian Sea has been affected by oil seepage; 1.5 million hectares of Kazak land was 'virtually destroyed' by missile launch emissions of heptyl.[48] Both domestic and foreign investors with an interest in such plants are having to close or repair the facilities which do not conform to currently acceptable standards.

Mention has already been made of the degradation of steppe during the 'Virgin Lands Campaign' in northern Kazakstan; the degradation of grassland was widespread, especially after the enforced collectivization of nomadic Kazaks.[49] Stalin's

---

[45] From 1949 until 1963 there were 124 nuclear explosions above ground, followed by 343 underground tests, inducing atmospheric fall-out or underground water pollution.
[46] The Koreans were from the Far East in districts bordering Manchuria and Korea (both then Japanese-occupied), and Stalin obsessively feared they would collaborate in the event of invasion. Their settlement in Uzbekistan brought an expansion of rice cultivation and is likely to remain permanent.
[47] UNDP, *Kazakstan Human Development Report 1996*, p. 99: the republic average was 102 kg.
[48] Murray Feshbach, *Ecological Disaster: Cleaning Up the Hidden Legacy of the Soviet Regime*, Twentieth Century Fund, New York, 1995, pp. 56, 58 and 73.
[49] A description of the problem in neighbouring countries of Inner Asia is in Caroline Humphrey and David Sneath (eds), *Culture and Environment in Inner Asia*, Vol. 1: *The Pastoral Economy and the Environment*, White Horse Press, Cambridge, 1996, esp. chs 3 (by Chen Shan) and 7 (by E. Erdenijab).

wildly misdirected 'Plan for the Transformation of Nature' liquidated many of the nature reserves set up under the provisions of Lenin's decree of 1921, but the network was subsequently re-established and expanded. There are three designated 'biosphere reserves' in Kazakstan and four in Uzbekistan, three of which straddle borders with other CIS states.[50] Intra-CIS collaboration is especially necessary in the protection of water supplies (discussed in Chapter 4), and it has been argued that more could be done by mobilizing public opinion in networks proper to a civil society.[51]

[50] For a map and brief history, see *The Encyclopedia of Russia and the Former Soviet Union*, Cambridge University Press, Cambridge, 1994, pp. 300–1.
[51] Douglas Saltmarshe, 'Civil Society and Sustainable Development in Central Asia', *Central Asian Survey*, Vol. 15, No. 3/4, 1996, pp. 387–98.

2 TRANSFORMING THE ECONOMIC SYSTEM

Presidential objectives

The schemes now being implemented for systemic change in the two republics have much in common. In a speech in Washington in February 1994, President Nursultan Nazarbayev declared that

> the development of democracy, property rights reform and the movement towards a full-fledged market system have been recognized as the sole means of lifting the economy out of crisis and are creating a climate conducive to the rise of a nation state. In pursuing this course, we must soberly assess existing realities, eschewing any exalted breakthroughs. We must adopt a calm and measured pragmatism. In implementing the transformation process we must take into account the existing psychology and traditions of the people, with due consideration for the rudiments of the former totalitarian regime in both our consciousness and our deeds, from which we cannot quickly free ourselves no matter how much we may wish to do so.[1]

President Islam Karimov stressed the need both for thorough change and for a gradual implementation:

> Centralized planning and market economies are two integrated, inherently logical and, hence, absolutely incompatible economic systems. Because of this, [a] planned economy cannot be transformed straightaway into a market one. The transition ... means the establishment of something principally new: transition from one qualitative state into another ... Thus, it cannot be implemented with a single act, but presupposes a sufficiently protracted period characterized by a sequence of stages.[2]

---

[1] Nursultan Nazarbayev, *A Strategy for the Development of Kazakhstan as a Sovereign State*, Kazakstan Embassy, Washington, DC, 1994.
[2] Islam Karimov, *Building the Future: Uzbekistan – Its Own Model for Transition to a Market Economy*, Uzbekistan Publishers, Tashkent, 1993, p. 56.

As policy guidelines, four of President Karimov's Basic Principles concern the economy (the other is supremacy of the rule of law):

(1)   the priority of economic policy over politics;
(2)   the state guarantees economic transformation;
(3)   social protection as a major function of the state;
(4)   the consistent and phased implementation of economic reforms.

These aims have been formulated as the 'Uzbek Model' of systemic transition, differing from the late Soviet expectations of 'market socialism' and from 'shock therapy' in six principles:[3]

(1)   creation of organized competitive markets with all the powers of the state;
(2)   commercialization of economic activity, accomplishing the transformation of monopoly structures into organized competitive markets;
(3)   utilization of market structures and technical restructuring as mutually supportive elements for the modernization of the economy;
(4)   privatization not as an end in itself but as a means of assuring competition and economic incentives;
(5)   influencing emerging institutions by an organized competitive market or by the assurance of such competition;
(6)   establishment of market reforms such that everyone gains without worsening the situation of others.

Governments in both states may be interpreted as being guided by two key criteria: first, the 'visible hand' of the state is accorded a prominent role in marketization; and, secondly, reform outcomes should be egalitarian. In practical terms social equality may be achieved by subsidies to restructuring firms to prevent labour redundancy, by maintaining the real value of child allowances, education and pensions in a country with a high dependency ratio, by dispersing new investment to equilibrate regional levels of living and by keeping peasants on egalitarian dividends from cooperatives rather than allowing income differentials to widen under independent farming (59 per cent of Uzbekistan's population and 41 per cent of Kazakstan's live in rural areas).

---

[3] A Deputy Prime Minister, Viktor Chzhen, also Chairman of the State Property Committee, uses the term 'The Uzbek Model of Privatization' (*Pravda Vostoka*, 8 August 1995) and Gul'nara Karimova, *Politiko-ekonomicheskie reformy v Uzbekistane: realii i perspektivy*, 1995, writes of 'The Uzbekistan Model'. The six tenets cited here are from her book (p. 22).

The 'shock' of 1992

While they renounced 'shock therapy', governments underwent a financial shock at the very moment of independence. Within the Soviet system the net transfers from central funds to Union Republics equilibrated not only the balance-of-payments surplus (as already mentioned), but also the Union Republican budget and, within it, local authority budgets. Union transfers to Kazakstan in 1991 were 4.5 per cent of GDP and to Uzbekistan 18.5 per cent; in 1992, the first full year of independence, the latter got nothing, but the former received transitional help of 1.8 per cent of GDP.[4] But simultaneously with the termination of that grant, government revenue declined (principally as tax collection failed to track the changing tax base, but also as state enterprises cut output and closed or accumulated tax arrears), and expenditure rose (mainly as the same recession evoked subsidies to state firms, consumer-price support, and higher social payments). In 1992 in Uzbekistan a huge deficit of 18 per cent of GDP separated a diminished revenue of 31 per cent and an increased expenditure of 43 per cent of GDP; adding the deficit on the external sector and on extrabudgetary funds (such as the Social Security Fund), the deficit was 18 per cent of GDP. Partly because Union transfers had been smaller to Kazakstan, the 1992 deficit, including extrabudgetary funds, was only 7 per cent of GDP, but the magnitude was also manageable because revenue held up and expenditure was trimmed. The following year Uzbek tax receipts improved (to 42 per cent of GDP), but expenditure continued to take more resources (62 per cent of GDP) and the deficit remained high – 20 per cent for the budget alone and 12 per cent on the broader definition.

Confronted by such a 'shock', the two governments had no option but to monetize those deficits: there was no financial market on which they could borrow, the issue of Soviet roubles remained unrestricted and the tax system would take time and determination to restructure. In the absence also of cheques, credit and debit cards and electronic money transmission, the increase in the money supply went straight into a cash inflation. There were other factors in the hyperinflation of 1992 and 1993, when the annual percentage increments in wholesale prices were respectively 3,275 and 2,545 in Uzbekistan and 2,369 and 1,340 in Kazakstan. Of these factors, four were common to both states:

(1)   Most wholesale prices were decontrolled in January 1992 (as they were throughout the CIS): state enterprises took advantage of their dominant market positions to push output prices ahead of input prices – there were few producers in any branch, as it was Soviet practice to seek economies of scale, and many supplies from outside the republic were disrupted;

---

[4] *IMF Economic Reviews: Kazakhstan,* April 1995, p. 49; IMF Staff Country Report 95/23, p. iv.

(2)   Import costs were raised by rouble depreciation (180 to the dollar in January 1992 and 1,181 in November 1993, when the link was snapped to create the tenge and the sum), which reflected currency risk, capital flight, external debt and foreign trade deficits (which all rouble area countries ran in 1992 and/or 1993);

(3)   Unit labour costs rose because workers were not laid off as sales volumes fell and social costs increased (the employer paid social insurance premia and from mid-1992 in Uzbekistan a supplementary 3 per cent of wage bills for a new Employment Fund, and a year later in Kazakstan a supplementary 2 per cent);

(4)   Privatization was initially slow and state firms exercised their monopoly power, as did partners in other CIS states.

Uzbekistan undertook a course of greater protection to the consumer. First, retail prices were partially decontrolled. This meant that the rise in the consumer price index was smaller than that just noted in wholesale prices (the increments were 645 and 534 per cent in 1992 and 1993), and inflationary subsidies were paid to compensate producers for the rises in input prices and in wages. Secondly, to give recipients of state-enterprise wages and of social payments access to consumer goods at subsidized prices in state shops, a few goods were rationed and 'coupons' were issued (one per rouble for 70 per cent of the payment): money – including large previously unspent household balances – unaccompanied by coupons flooded the market, especially the private sector, and gave inflation a further push.

A political economy of gradualism

Both presidents, each of whom had been the Union Republican Party leader at the break-up of the USSR, were sharply aware of the danger of popular unrest. There had been nationalist riots with fatalities when President Nazarbayev's predecessor, Gennady Kolbin, a Russian, had been nominated in December 1986, displacing an ethnic Kazak. Nazarbayev himself had been appointed in June 1989 in the wake of riots sparked by unemployment and disputes over housing. Karimov took office as Uzbek Party leader in June 1989, too, at the time of the massacre of Meskhetians by Fergana Valley Uzbeks, which left a hundred dead and a thousand injured. A year later (June 1990) hundreds had been killed in Osh (Kyrgyzstan) in conflicts started by the expropriation of a large part of the land of a collective farm held by minority Uzbeks: continuing inter-ethnic unrest led to the installation of the current president, Askar Akayev, in November 1990. Nazarbayev has had close contact with the warring sides in Tajikistan, intervening in November 1992 during a lull in the civil war to assure a peaceful transition in the presidency from Rahmon Nabiev to

Emomali Rakhmonov.[5] Uzbekistan is still more profoundly concerned with the long-running hostilities in Tajikistan. At home President Karimov was confronted with civil disorder, repressed only with fatalities, after the January 1992 price decontrol and attempts to reduce expenditure by cuts in student grants. He then gained political advantage by blaming the riots on his rival, Shukrulla Mirsaidov, and on the liberal and Islamic opposition parties, and by introducing rationing and a coupon system (described above, p. 25) for subsidized consumer goods.

Each president thus had reason to fear that his political authority could be threatened by further shocks to living standards and in any event needed time to consolidate his position as a national leader. In the early years of independence, therefore, they were both averse to loosening the state's economic controls. An equally powerful factor in delaying economic change was the time they needed to counter regional power-centres. Attention has been drawn above to the threefold division of the ethnic Kazaks and to the substantial numbers of Russians who until 1986 had been the largest single nationality. Even at independence, 48 per cent of the population of Kazakstan were ethnic Europeans – Slavs and the deported populations of Stalin's repression (notably Germans and Poles). The 15,000 Russian protesters calling for dual nationality and equal status for the Russian language (Ust-Kamenogorsk, December 1992) showed the strength of irredentism. Under laws of 1989 in Uzbekistan and 1993 in Kazakstan Russian is a lingua franca alongside the official Uzbek or Kazak, but the effects of recent modifications in the status of Russian remain to be seen. The linguistic compromises, however, helped to provide political space for economic reform.

In Uzbekistan the ethnic problem – Uzbeks and Tajiks (as already mentioned in Chapter 1, p. 14 – is quantitatively smaller than in Kazakstan, but there is the quadripartite and potentially divisive regional subdivision – from west to east, Karakalpakstan, Bukhara-Samarkand, Tashkent and the Fergana Valley. The first of these was an independent khanate (Khiva) even throughout Tsarist times and was incorporated into Soviet administration as late as 1923; it had special status as an Autonomous Republic within the Uzbek SSR. Since Uzbek independence its Parliament Chairman, Ubbiniyaz Ashirbekov, is the only one of the 13 regional leaders to have remained in place; President Karimov, himself a Samarkandi, personally went to the regional assembly of Samarkand in November 1995 to advocate dismissal of the last of those who had not already been replaced. In fact, Samarkand Region represents the type of alliance the presidential regime has formed between

---

[5] Dilip Hiro, *Between Marx and Muhammad*. HarperCollins, London, 1995, pp. 112–15, 132 and 220. See also Yuri Kulchik, Andrey Fadin and Victor Sergeev, *Central Asia after the Empire*, Pluto Press, London, 1996, ch. 4.

burgeoning private entrepreneurs and the local political leadership. Under a political boss from the Soviet period, the police and other authorities had subjected businessmen to harassment and extortion: Karimov replaced the leadership, putting in a political heavyweight, Alisher Mardiev, Minister of Justice, as *hokim* (governor) to implement the political-economic alliance.

But if rapid marketization – the so-called 'shock therapy' – was renounced in the two states by the primacy of political centralization, it was only in the 'Uzbek model' (described above) that the essence was 'creation of organized markets with all the powers of the state.' Until 1994 President Nazarbayev pursued a more liberalizing course. Because he sought to emulate the practices of the central and east European states, he embraced voucher privatization early (in two separate waves). However, aspects of the implementation of this policy brought it into some disrepute, and changes of ministers in charge of the process added to the problem. Since 1994 there has been greater convergence in the two presidents' policies, through a form of dual economy. One tier of the economy is small-scale, labour-intensive and largely insider-owned. This was enlarged (it had never disappeared under the command economy, but rather filled its interstices) by privatization – a voucher distribution in Kazakstan and employee buy-outs in Uzbekistan – for small and medium-sized industry. State and collective farms were switched to 'closed shareholding companies' lacking ownership of their land. The other tier of the economy – mining, bigger manufacturing, wholesaling and banking – is mostly either state-run or in state minority shareholding in a joint venture with a foreign multinational. Foreigners are not players in domestic politics, save in lobbying in their own interest; expatriates who transgress the political norms can be excluded from the country. Current conditions favour capital inflow, for the external position is strengthening. Foreign implants generate marketable products and the government is determined that they operate in partnership with a continuingly strong public sector.

Inflation and the new currencies

If political considerations dictated extreme gradualism in economic transformation, the tying of both countries to the Russian rouble until November 1993 complicated any accompanying passage to financial stability. As already noted, the two governments monetized the budget deficits subsequent to the Soviet break-up, but whereas Uzbekistan used claims on the rouble to expand its money supply, 'for Kazakstan, inflation was mainly exogenous, reflecting the stance of monetary policy in the rouble zone as a whole ... Kazakstan refrained from taking a "free ride" in the rouble zone'.[6]

---

[6] *IMF Economic Reviews: Kazakhstan*, April 1995, p. 2.

It was also the case that in a simplistic approach to disinflationary instruments the Kazak Central Bank restricted the issue of banknotes at an early stage: the cash-to-deposit ratio touched a nadir of 27 per cent at the end of June 1992; Uzbekistan took action later and, coincidentally, reached a nadir of the same ratio of 27 per cent in December 1993.[7] The IMF, which Kazakstan had joined in July, and Uzbekistan in September 1992, warned the newly independent states of the difficulties of managing their own currencies, and for a time argued for continued use of the rouble throughout the CIS; other advisers proposed a clearing union; and a few saw the rouble as a basis for a reintegrated Soviet economic space. The Baltic states and Ukraine had left the rouble zone in 1992, but it was in the summer of 1993 that the radical division came. In May Kyrgyzstan launched its own currency unit, the som, and simultaneously gained a stand-by arrangement with the IMF (of $38 million[8]), but the general exodus happened in July when the Central Bank of Russia demonetized pre-1993 roubles and offered new currency only if it controlled the partner's credit supply and reserves: all save Tajikistan chose separation. In the two republics the Kazak tenge and the Uzbek sum-coupon became the sole legal tender in November 1993.

Kazakstan quickly undertook negotiations with the IMF for the support of a permanent currency and in January 1994 obtained a stand-by arrangement with the IMF of $173 million. The agreement required a tightening of monetary policy and a move towards positive real interest rates, but once the stand-by agreement was obtained the Kazak government decided to net out inter-enterprises arrears by budget-financed bank credit. This reversed the downward trend in inflation, and the fiscal deficit rocketed to 18 per cent of GDP in the first quarter and 15 per cent in the second quarter. Advice from the IMF was conducive to a reinforcement of financial policies from July 1994, and a wide-ranging liberalization of prices was undertaken; the full-year outcome for the budget deficit was down to 6.8 per cent of GDP. In 1995 that deficit was cut to 2.3 per cent of GDP and the IMF commented that the year 'was the most successful for the Kazak economy since independence. Inflation was reduced significantly and the balance of payments performed significantly better than expected.'[9] There was a real depreciation of the tenge (the fall in the exchange rate exceeding inflation), which encouraged imports. Rewarding the Action Programme for the Deepening of Reforms, the IMF approved in July 1996 a three-year credit under the Extended Fund Facility of $446 million. The programme envisaged an upturn in overall economic activity that year – as indeed eventuated – and bigger increments to

---

[7] Daniel Hardy and Ashok Lahiri, 'Cash Shortage in the Former Soviet Union', *Journal of Comparative Economics*, Vol. 22, No. 2, April 1996, pp. 119–40.

[8] IMF accounting is designated in Special Drawing Rights (SDR); the values cited are converted at the Fund's stated rates to the US dollar.

[9] *IMF Survey*, 29 July 1996, p. 256; the account of 1994–5 is chiefly from *IMF Economic Reviews: Kazakhstan*, 1994, pp. 3–4.

Table 2: Comparative indicators of macroeconomic stability in the CIS

CIS state	Inflation in 1994	Inflation in 1996	Budget deficit 1994	Budget deficit 1996
Armenia	1,885	19	-16	-8
Azerbaijan	1,788	15	-15	-3
Belarus	1,957	61	-3	-2
Georgia	7,144	23	-7	-4
Kazakstan	**1,160**	**26**	**-7**	**-4**
Kyrgyzstan	87	27	-8	-6
Moldova	45	26	-9	-4
Russia	203	25	-10	-6
Tajikistan	5	200	-11	-6
Turkmenistan	1,330	250	-1*	...
Ukraine	401	55	-8	-7
Uzbekistan	**1,281**	**35**	**-6**	**-4**

Source: EBRD, *Transition Report 1996*, pp. 113. Cols 1 and 2 are indices of consumer price infla-tion as percentage change at end of year; cols 3 and 4 are general government (i.e. central, region-al and local) balances for the year as percentage of GDP; 1996 values are EBRD forecasts.
* Information on both revenue and expenditure is partial.

GDP in 1997 and 1998 (respectively 0.9 and 2.8 per cent).

Uzbekistan was initially less cooperative with the IMF.[10] Discussions begun in February 1994 were broken off in May and the transfer from the sum-coupon to the sum was independently introduced. The new unit was exchangeable for 1,000 sum-coupons without restriction (save for a short delay in converting bank balances), on 1 July, at seven to the dollar. The elimination of three noughts had a cosmetic effect, and may have concealed from the general public a near-halving of the external value: in April and May, following a partial abolition of current-account controls, the sum-coupon had been steady at around 3,700 to the dollar, though it dropped to 4,600 in June. The Central Bank of Uzbekistan judged that it had enough foreign-exchange reserves ($700 million) and gold ($440 million) to float the sum, but, reflecting continued inflation and anticipated currency risk, it plunged. By mid-October it was at 20 to the dollar, less than a fifth of its external value five months before. Only one anti-inflationary measure was adopted – a 100 per cent tax (until the end of the year) on wage-bill increments that exceeded 70 per cent of any

---

[10] An informative comparison of the introduction of the sum-coupon and of the Kyrgyz som, respec-tively with and without IMF advice, is in Makkamjan Abdoulkadyrov, 'Monetary Reform: A Comparison of the Kyrgyz Republic and the Republic of Uzbekistan', *Comparative Economic Studies*, Vol. 37, No. 3, Fall 1995, pp. 39–56; 'the continued easy credit and monetary policies of the Central Bank' (p. 44) were a patent factor in Uzbekistan's failure.

month's sales. But in the medium term other market-liberalizing measures helped to eliminate consumer-goods subsidies; rationing was limited to flour, sugar and vegetable oils and retail price controls were set much higher maxima for bread, flour, household utilities and urban transport. Though this reduced the inflationary effect of subsidies, prices rose rapidly and wages followed. President Karimov, in a populist gesture, awarded direct payments to virtually every adult to offset the price rise – 100 sum (from November 150) – as a monthly supplement to wages and social benefits. The state-owned commercial banks were allowed to go on subsidizing enterprises at negative interest rates, and some were subsidized still further by permission to buy imports at a concessional exchange rate. That discount was at the expense of exporters, who from April 1994 had to sell 30 per cent of their foreign currency receipts to the Central Bank at the official (rather than the market) exchange rate. Consumer prices (1,568 per cent for 1994 as a whole) almost caught up with wholesale prices (1,428 per cent), and the fiscal deficit, 12 per cent of GDP in 1993, and budgeted for 3.5 per cent in 1994, was in the event 7 per cent.

The authorities then realized that they could not manage without the IMF and in January 1995 signed their first agreement. A systemic transformation facility of $74 million was negotiated against a programme of reducing the fiscal deficit to 3.5 per cent of GDP (of which 2 per cent was funded by domestic banks) and, with privatization and income policy measures, cutting inflation down to 84 per cent for the year 1995. The deficit target was virtually met (at 4 per cent of GDP), but inflation was not tamed so fast; the annual average was 315 per cent. The foreign-exchange market was stabilized and a major liberalization of exchange controls was applied, including the lifting of restrictions on individuals' purchase of foreign currency. In fact the real rate of exchange – the actual change in the nominal rate (from 22 to 36 during 1995) deflated by price rises in the home and the marker-currency countries – substantially appreciated. The IMF was sufficiently impressed to repeat the systemic transformation facility (in the same $74 million) and to add $259 million as a stand-by credit. As agreed in December 1995, the programme requires the decline in economic activity to be restricted to 1.5 per cent in 1996, inflation to be down to 21–25 per cent and the fiscal deficit to be unchanged at 4 per cent. But proportionately less of that deficit would be met from the Central Bank (by printing money) and more by borrowing from commercial banks and eventually by issuing treasury bonds. In the event, though negative growth was less (-1.2 per cent of GDP), inflation was insufficiently lowered and the IMF suspended disbursement of its credit.

Together with the targets for aggregative relationships, the IMF encouraged the two governments to restructure their revenue and expenditure towards a market environment. Value-added tax had been introduced and in 1995 generated 12 per cent of Kazak revenue and 19 per cent of the Uzbek; personal income tax (which had been trivial in the Soviet system) raised respectively 11 and 9 per cent; excise duties in Kazakstan (excluding a levy on cotton), brought in 3 per cent, against 5 per cent in Uzbekistan. On the expenditure side the heavy 'national economy' entry, burdened with state investment and subsidies to enterprises in Soviet practice, was down to 17 per cent in Kazakstan and 13 per cent in Uzbekistan; social expenditure had increased against 1992 (37 against 33 per cent) in Kazakstan and was virtually at the same proportion (36 against 37 per cent) in Uzbekistan. President Nazarbayev survived an effective vote of no confidence when he obtained the assent of parliament, the Kenges, in July 1996 to cut annual pension expenditure by raising the retirement age by three years.[11]

Market reform and privatization

The programmes agreed with the IMF also had, as normally in such circumstances, institutional parameters. Thus, the agreement with the Uzbek government in December 1995 required the government 'to add momentum to its structural reform efforts, with particular emphasis on the privatization of medium- and large-scale enterprises, enterprise reform, continued liberalization of foreign trade, and further disengagement of the government in economic activity'.[12] Small-scale private activity, both legal and illicit, had been quite developed in both countries, even if before perestroika the bazaar had been a shadow of itself under the New Economic Policy of the 1920s.[13]

Uzbek privatization had been enacted a mere seven weeks after the declaration of independence in a Law on Destatization and Privatization, whereby state productive assets were placed in the hands of a State Property Committee; it had earlier the same year established the legal bases for non-state enterprise by Laws on Enterprises and on Entrepreneurship (February 1991) and on Cooperatives (June 1991). The State Property Committee – later 'and Privatization' (DKI) – was made responsible for the privatization programme and for foreign participation therein. There was, however, a long delay before actual property transfers began, as in all transition states, with the sale of small trade and service outlets and housing. The proportion of housing in private ownership had been the highest in the USSR. Householders

[11] *Caspian Brief*, Vol. 1, No. 2, 1996.
[12] Press Release of 18 December 1995, *IMF Survey*, 8 January 1996, p. 17.
[13] A fascinating account, recently reprinted in translation, of a contemporary journey through Uzbekistan is Ella Maillart, *Turkestan Solo*, Century Hutchison, London, and Orpen, Toronto, 1988; she also describes the subjugation of women (including wearing of the head-to-toe *paranja*) on the very eve of emancipation. The present writer's impression of the Tashkent and Samarkand bazaars in 1957 was during the spring, when animal fodder was a principal commodity and foodstuffs at an annual nadir.

were given (within certain limits) ownership of the property they occupied, although not of the land on which it stood. The transfer is now virtually complete.

The options open, under the 1991 Law, were leasing, transformation into a co-operative, sale by auction and sale by tender. No formal preference was accorded employees, but Article 6 specifically encouraged it and authorized the use of retained profits and even of the amortization fund for a group buy-out. Furthermore, control is exercised through share ownership by insiders of at least 25 per cent of equity (including any held by the State Property Fund). Transfer was intense during 1993: through the GKI the Ministry of Trade divested itself of nearly all its retail outlets, and the Ministry of Health of non-hospital pharmacies and opticians; outside the GKI schemes, regional *hokimiyats* disposed of their various small establishments.[14] Together with earlier- and newly-established private entities, there were in Uzbekistan 83,500 small-scale private enterprises on 1 July 1996. Retail sales during the first half of 1996 were only 6.2 per cent generated in the wholly state sector, with 2.4 per cent in joint ventures, 66.9 per cent in private hands, and 21.9 per cent in the collective (mainly farm) sector.[15]

Large-scale privatization was embodied in a Presidential Decree of March 1994. No vouchers were on offer and foreign buyers have been welcomed, either to bid at auction or to negotiate individual purchase. Preparation for the sale of large enterprises included in 1994 the establishment of the Tashkent Stock Exchange, a National Share Depository and a National Investment Fund, and the engagement of Price Waterhouse as advisers. The first auctions of medium-sized enterprises were held in April and May 1994, and included some substantial hotels: the prestigious Registan Hotel in Samarkand went for 75 billion sum-coupons ($19 million at the then rate of exchange). The biggest purchase to date has been by BAT of the United Kingdom of a share in a tobacco joint venture, described in Chapter 4 (p. 45). A large number of production branches will be unaffected – cotton plantations, the energy, metals, mining, pharmaceutical and 'high-technology' industries, and railway and air transport. The Commission of the European Union financed (900,000 ECU) three of the first sell-offs to test and establish procedures, and its staff remain in an advisory capacity. On 1 July 1996, 25.4 per cent of enterprises remained in state ownership, but they produced 49.8 per cent of domestic goods and services; their higher labour productivity (for they include the technologically more advanced 'excluded industries') put their employment at 29.9 per cent of the national total. A Presidential Decree of July 1996 envisaged an acceleration in privatization.

---

[14] *Investment Guide for Uzbekistan*, UNDP and OECD, Paris, 1996, p. 34.
[15] These and other ownership statistics at 1 July 1996 are from *Basic Results of Social and Economic Development of Uzbekistan*, January–June 1996.

The Kazak government differentiated its three non-farm privatization schemes (small business, mass privatization and housing) from other CIS governments' by choosing vouchers denominated in points rather than money, and by the compulsory use of investment funds rather than direct purchase of equity; reportedly it drew initial inspiration for an all-citizen voucher distribution from the example of neighbouring Mongolia. It also took steps to assure to 'outsiders' control of privatized enterprises, which in most other members of the CIS went to 'insiders', and to attract foreign capital into the controlling equity. It had been the first Union Republic to create its own State Property Committee (January 1991) and began small privatization as early as August 1991. On attaining independence at the end of that year, the government formulated principles for voucher privatization, which operated until January 1996 with the following characteristics.

(1)   Of the two forms of privatization cheque, that designated an 'investment coupon' was distributed to all citizens, those in rural areas receiving 120 points and those in urban areas 100 points. Distribution of coupons took place in late 1993.

(2)   By closure at end January 1996 1,692 billion points had been issued; auctions had taken 1,127 billion points to buy into 1,688 enterprises (of which 732 still had a 51 per cent state holding, 339 had 25–51 per cent and 617 less than 25 per cent).[16]

(3)   Investment coupons could only be deposited in 'investment privatization funds' and could not be traded or used directly to buy equity. So few coupons had been deposited in funds (a mere 15 per cent had been redeemed at the seven auctions by November 1994) that the government was compelled to waive deadlines for deposit and to offer a money value first of 4 roubles and then one tenge per point (a derisory offer, when a litre of petrol then cost 6 tenge officially, and 12 tenge on the open market).

(4)   By January 1996, 169 investment privatization funds had been established, and had accumulated 66 per cent of all points. The staff of many were inexperienced; they gave exaggerated estimates of early profits; sought to evade the legal provisions on a 37 per cent maximum holding in any one enterprise (by creating a multiplicity of subsidiaries to buy into an enterprise); formed auction 'rings'; and allegedly had 'spies' in the State Property Committee.[17]

(5)   The other form of privatization cheque is the housing coupon, the aggregate value distributed to citizens being equal to the estimated value of the public

[16] *Kazakstan Economic Trends*, February 1996, pp. 94–5.
[17] *Labyrinth*, Vol. 1, No. 3, Summer 1995, pp. 14–5. Funds formed themselves into rival groups.

housing stock. Because many rebates were given on the estimated value of dwellings, and some tenants opted not to buy their accommodation, more than half of these coupons remained unspent, and were converted into investment coupons (although the government had expected them to be used for 'small privatization').

The differentiation between urban and rural recipients could be ostensibly to compensate for different levels of living; it could also have been to promote President Nazarbayev's image among the 43 per cent of rural voters. But a more apposite comment is that ethnic Kazaks are predominantly countryfolk and Russianized Kazaks, Russians and Ukrainians live in the northern towns.

In a Decree on the National Privatization Programme (March 1993), state enterprises were classed into three groups: 'small privatization' applied to the 5,000 businesses with fewer than 200 workers; 'mass privatization' to the 850 firms with between 200 and 5,000 staff; and case-by-case privatization to the 100 enterprises with more than 5,000 employees (of which 25 were subsequently listed as open for a controlling foreign purchase, including the important oil and gas industries). The first step in the procedure was corporatization and, for the medium-sized and large enterprises, the establishment of state holding companies (34 were created, covering three-quarters of industrial production) holding the government's equity. The aim was not so much devolution as the assurance by ownership of previous contractual supply-sales relations. Difficulties arose because employees had unexpired leases on the equipment and challenged the legality of the sale, or because managers of the corporatized business who had been underbidders removed equipment before formal handover and had to be pursued through the courts. But by 1 January 1995 there were 11,464 small enterprises in private ownership.

In the medium-size category 10 per cent of the equity is passed to the employees, 51 per cent is available for purchase by an investment privatization fund, and 39 per cent remains state property. The State Property Committee has not restructured enterprises before offering them at auction and many sales have not gone through because of the enterprise's heavy indebtedness: chiefly concerned with reducing the budget deficit in the interest of disinflation, the government has not made restructuring finance available. The total at 1 January 1996 in this private-sector category was 21,260.

Large enterprises are being sold individually, KPMG advising the State Privatization Committee. Although employees were until January 1996 assured a 10 per cent stake, as in smaller enterprises, the majority share is available. Foreign purchasers are welcome and Kazakstan is second only to Russia in the CIS in attracting them, as Chapter 3 recounts. Unlike in Uzbekistan (and Turkmenistan),

Table 3: Privatization in Kazakstan (percentage of enterprises)

Branch	1994	1995	2000 slow variant	2000 fast variant
Industry & mining	17	25	30–35	35–40
Agriculture	46	50	57–62	63–67
Trade & catering	50	65	80–85	85–90
Business services	11	28	60–65	65–70
Consumer services	51	63	75–85	85–90

Source: Yelena Kalyuzhnova, *The Privatization of Property in the Republic of Kazakstan*, University of Reading Department of Economics, Discussion Papers in Economics, No. 319, August 1995. Data for 1995 are provisional and in agriculture no farm is included in which some share is state-owned.

hydrocarbons are not excluded from privatization. The long-established Emba oil industry was set up for privatization in 1995, with Western advisers, and the huge new oil and gas deposits are being developed with Western partners, as also shown in Chapter 3. As in Uzbekistan, the state may maintain a substantial holding in a joint venture with a foreign firm. A senior official in the Department of Economic Policy of the Kazakstan Council of Ministers explained this preference as allowing monitoring by a government agency as co-owner in a medium-term perspective.[18] By January 1996, of the 180 large firms scheduled for privatization, transfer had been completed for only five.

The privatization process was radically restructured in January 1996. Preferential property treatment for staff was abolished, leaving only two channels of privatization – direct sale to investors and auctions. The social guarantees previously required of buyers of state enterprises will no longer be demanded, but a criterion among applicants to buy will be the terms they set out for restructuring (the 'business plan'), just as the Treuhandanstalt required in East German privatization. The programme to the end of the century (Table 3) has two scenarios, with fewer transfers envisaged if privatization is reactive to purchaser demand and more if the authorities are more proactive.[19]

In tandem with privatization and the influx of foreign enterprise, the Kazak government is actively promoting an indigenous private sector. A 'State Programme for

[18] Marat Rysbekov (Chief, Privatization Section), 'Privatization in Kazakhstan', *Comparative Economic Studies*, Vol. 37, No. 3, Fall 1995, pp. 1–10.
[19] Yelena Kalyuzhnova, *The Privatization of Property in the Republic of Kazakstan*, University of Reading Department of Economics, Discussion Papers in Economics, No. 319, August 1995, pp. 15–17 (embodiment in the 1996 law confirmed by personal communication).

Table 4: Privatization in Uzbekistan (percentage of sales in first half of 1996)

Branch	State	Private	Corporate	Joint venture	Other
Industry and mining	49.8	..	..	..	..
Agriculture	4.9	68.4	5.0	0.0	21.7
Trade & catering	6.2	69.3	5.6	2.4	16.5
Consumer services	71.0	12.7	9.6	0.0	6.7
Aggregate net material product	56.2	16.8	17.1	2.2	7.7

Source: *Basic Results of Social and Economic Development of the Republic of Uzbekistan*, January–June 1996, Tashkent. The source does not distinguish between categories of non-state owner in industry and mining; 0.0 means less than 0.1 per cent.

Supporting and Encouraging Enterprise in Kazakstan', promulgated in July 1994, requires completion of the legal and financial infrastructure of a developed market economy, based on the inviolability and protection of private property: there is room, it asserts, for 150,000 private businesses in Kazakstan.[20] Soviet law had permitted private prospecting teams to mine for gold.[21] In Kazakstan, as in Russia, these teams took over the small deposits which had been attributed to them and formed their own joint-stock companies. The Zarya *artel'*, then with two mines, is now the Balkhash Company with six mines, 2,400 staff and two ore-processing plants producing gold 'dore' of 90 per cent purity.[22]

In both countries privatization has been accompanied by accusations of favouritism towards individuals and towards the titular ethnic group. Cronyism and corruption merging into organized crime are certainly present in many property transfers of post-Soviet states and hinder the foreign participation which could bring managerial and physical restructuring. As noted above, the *hokim* of Samarkand was dismissed on such charges. In response to protests that ethnic Kazaks were being crowded out of small privatization, the government provided special funds to enable such people to make purchases. The mass public protest in Almaty of October 1996 (noted in Chapter 3) was partly a response to corrupt privatization.

---

[20] Kirill Nourzhanov and Amin Saikal, 'The New Kazakhstan: Has Something Gone Wrong?' *The World Today*, December 1994, p. 227.

[21] Michael Kaser, 'The Soviet Gold-Mining Industry', in R.G. Jensen, T. Shabad and A.W. Wright (eds), *Soviet Natural Resources in the World Economy*, University of Chicago Press, Chicago, 1983, esp. pp. 583–4.

[22] CBI, *Doing Business in Kazakstan*, p. xvii.

Agrarian restructuring

An American analyst saw, early on, four currents in Kazakstan on agrarian reform. In the immediate aftermath of independence she perceived the 'free marketeers' as having influence (conceptually near them were 'pragmatic marketeers' envisaging the maintenance of some state regulation), but later giving way to 'neo-collectivists' in which the voice of existing farm management dominated (with an offshoot in 'market socialists' proposing the reorganization of state and collective farms into associations of smaller private farms).[23] Events seem to have confirmed her perception. Under legislation of 1991 land could be leased for up to 99 years as saleable and heritable, but not mortgageable; such leaseholds, together with household plots, already accounted the following year for one-third of the livestock and one half of plant output other than cotton and grain. But by March 1994 legislation was more oriented towards vested interests. The land of a cooperative or state farm, as a joint-stock company, may be divided into four tranches: 20 per cent may be bought by the director personally; 29 per cent is available for purchase by other members, employees and pensioners; 20 per cent is to be auctioned to buyers who must be Kazak citizens and have an education and work experience relevant to agriculture; and 31 per cent may be leased for a maximum of five years. The Kazak Private Farmers' Association welcomed the measure which buys off the *nomenklatura* opponents of agrarian reform – not only the director, but local officials who can buy in at auction or leasehold sale. The state procurement agency, Kazkhlebprodukt, was turned in January 1994 into a joint-stock company and its monopoly was withdrawn. Although in December 1994 the Premier, Akezhan Kazhegeldin, declared that parliament would be asked to legislate for full private ownership of land in the republic, no legislation has been enacted. By mid-1996, 90 per cent of collective and state farms (80 per cent of farmland) had been distributed into leaseholds or joint-stock companies. Agro-industrial enterprises, buying from or selling to farms, had nearly all been privatized into cooperatives, often associated with local farms.

For Uzbekistan a Land Law of 1989 authorized the leasing to farm households of the irrigated land of collective farms. A further Land Law of July 1990 authorized the leasing of land to private persons, heritable but with the state as freeholder. In 1991 the land of loss-making state farms (other than cotton plantations) was leased to staff or became collective farms. Between the enactment of the Law on *Dekhkan Farms* (July 1992) and November 1993 the land and assets of state farms were leased to staff either as cooperatives or as 'closed' joint-stock companies (i.e. shares not on offer to outsiders, but tradeable among insiders).[24] In 1995 only 3 per cent of

[23] Cynthia Ann Werner, 'A Preliminary Assessment of Attitudes toward the Privatization of Agriculture in Contemporary Kazakhstan,' *Central Asian Survey*, Vol. 13, No. 2, 1994, pp. 295–303.
[24] The food and agricultural situation to late 1994 is surveyed in Peter Craumer, *Rural and Agricultural Development in Uzbekistan*, FSS Key Paper, RIIA, London, 1995.

agricultural output came from the state sector, that is, farms owned by factories, experimental stations and nature reserves (in the first half of 1996 their share was 5 per cent because livestock, rather than arable, produce predominates). Considerable impetus was given by a decree of January 1996 which permitted the auction of land with rights of lifetime ownership and inheritance.[25] By 1 July 1996, 19,307 *dekhkan* independent leasehold farms were registered (a total of 294,700 ha), and produced 67 per cent of agricultural output in the first six months of that year. Individual plots in the state and cooperative sector produced 1 per cent and the residual collective farms 6 per cent.[26]

State procurement remains for cotton and some non-food crops in Uzbekistan, but the last such crop in Kazakstan, grain, was freed in 1995. In both countries government purchasing agencies are intended to operate strictly commercially; the Astyk company for grain in Kazakstan from January 1995 was to limit its purchasing to state-enterprise requirements, but its planned privatization was delayed. Uzbek compulsory procurement of the Soviet type was cut on independence from 100 per cent of cotton and grain, successively to 80, then to 65, and from the 1996 crop to 50 per cent (bought at 70 per cent of the world price for cotton and at 60 per cent for grain). As in Soviet times, local administrations had been forcing farms to deliver to the state more than the stipulated share at the low prices, but from 1996 they have been told to leave the farms to market the rest freely. Fruit and vegetable procurements (previously 50 per cent) have been abandoned. By a reduction in cotton plantations, some irrigated land is being turned over to food crops, but in early 1996 President Karimov called on local authorities to enforce good practice on cultivators; he commented that the grain yield had not increased between 1993 and 1995, even though 62 per cent of the grain area was irrigated, against only 33 per cent in 1993. Another good practice being reintroduced is cotton rotation with alfalfa.[27]

The Uzbek food-import bill is the biggest in Central Asia and the government's aim of raising food production is among its reasons for slow decontrol and high subsidization, against which the international economic agencies are currently arguing. An example of an indirect subsidy was the March 1996 moratorium until the year 2000 on interest payments on government loans incurred by farm enterprises that are not making a profit and the total remission of interest on those making serious losses.

---

[25] EBRD, *Transition Report 1996*, p. 183.

[26] *Basic Results...*, January–June 1996

[27] This practice restores nutrient to the soil, but was largely abandoned in the Soviet drive to use every irrigated hectare for cotton and to apply nutrients in chemical fertilizer (the leaching of which pollutes the run-off water). The ECE Secretariat, in the UN's first report on Central Asia, recommended alfalfa rotation as long ago as 1957 (*Economic Bulletin for Europe*, Vol. 9, No. 3, pp. 49–75).

38

Property rights and regulation

Both republics accord foreigners the same rights as citizens, but preclude proprietorship by foreign companies to land and to assets not applicable to their specific activity. Profits and capital can be repatriated freely from the operation of such investments. Sales of property to foreigners and the establishment of joint ventures are actively encouraged. A Concessions Law of September 1995 provided that foreigners could tender, or bid at auction, for exclusive rights to land for mining or other development; a comparison of concession laws in the CIS shows Uzbekistan offering the shortest term, 15 years, while Georgia offers 50; Kazak law limits exploration concessions to six years, but allows those for extraction up to 25 years.[28]

Property rights in Kazakstan were codified in the General Part of a new Civil Code, which entered into force on 1 March 1995. The various forms of property and rights in acquisition, termination and protection are defined; obligations and securities are covered. A revised banking law was confirmed by decree of 1995.[29] The Uzbek parliament, the Oliy Majlis, made considerable progress at its spring 1996 session, introducing laws on the Regulation of the Securities Market (importantly incorporating guarantees for investors on the stock market), on Joint-Stock Companies and the Protection of Shareholders' Rights (a revision of corporate governance regulation), on banking and on establishing free economic zones.

President Karimov, in a wide-ranging survey in August 1995 of the progress of systemic change,[30] wrote of the replacement of the 'monopolizing ration-distributing monster Gossnab [State Supply Committee] and its foster-child Uzkontrakttorg [Uzbek Contractual Trade Agency]'. To facilitate 'the necessary infrastructure for free market participation with equality of rights of goods producers, consumers and entrepreneurs', he listed the Republican Joint-Stock Association of Wholesale and Bourse Trade which established commodity exchanges and 'commercial intermediary companies' both centrally and in the provinces; a Chief Administration in the Ministry of Finance for Demonopolization and Control of Excess Monopoly Pricing (subsequently made an autonomous agency); and 'independent and responsible banks'.

[28] Commentaries on these laws are in ECE, *East-West Investment News*, Autumn/Winter 1994; Summer 1996 (for the length of concessions); and Autumn 1996.
[29] See *Doing Business in Kazakstan*, pp. 26–9.
[30] *Uzbekistan po puti uglubleniya ekonomicheskikh reform*, Lenizdat, St Petersburg, 1995, p. 73.

The banking system

Bank regulation is especially needed. A two-tier banking system quickly replaced the 'monobank' of the Gosbank structure – a Central Bank and commercial banks, of which those of the Soviet structure were transformed into wholly-owned joint-stock banks. The principal among the latter are Agroprombank, Alembank (the former Vneshekonombank), Turanbank, the People's Bank (the former Sberbank) and Kredsotsbank in Kazakstan; and Agroprombank, Promstroibank, the National Bank for Foreign Economic Activities (the former Vneshekonombank), Pakhta Bank (formerly Agroprombank), Promstroibank and People's Bank (formerly Sberbank) in Uzbekistan. The successor to the Sberbank USSR was later privatized as the People's Bank in Kazakstan, but has remained a government agency in Uzbekistan. Overall, the IMF characterized the Kazak system as a 'weak financial position of major, formally fully state owned banks, as well as the fragile position of newly emerging private banks'.[31] Banking in Uzbekistan is dominated by state-owned banks and by banks owned by government agencies, including ministries. The National Bank for Foreign Economic Activity is the largest and plays the leading role in the provision of external banking services to both state and private sectors. Pakhta Bank, as mentioned above, is supporting rural business, Promstroibank works with industry and construction, and People's Bank has a nationwide branch network for personal savings. New banks have been created by the government to serve specific sectors, such as Galla-Bank, Savdogarbank, Mevasabzavotbank and Tadbirkor (the name means 'Entrepreneur', being also focused on small business and private farms). Of the 30 commercial banks established and remaining by late 1996, however, only eight were private and two were joint ventures with foreign participation, one of which, dating from November 1995, is the Asaka Bank, jointly owned by the government and the Daewoo Corporation, mainly to service the motor industry. The other is the Dutch bank ABN Amro, licensed in 1996 as a joint venture (but only 50 per cent equity) with the state-owned National Bank for Foreign Economic Activity (30 per cent), the EBRD and International Finance Corporation (IFC). Overall, the number of banks had been reduced by compulsory liquidations of some with inadequate reserves or engaging in illegal activity.

The improvement of Uzbekistan's attractiveness for investment has in the past two months been severely checked by confusion in the Central Bank's management of foreign-exchange transactions and a split on policy advice between the Bank and the National Bank for Foreign Economic Activities. This cumulates to a general weakness of the banking sector. The Central Bank in April 1996 had to limit to 29 specified commercial banks the right to transact with individuals, commenting that

---

[31] IMF Country Study: *Kazakstan* 96/22, p. 38.

this was to warn the public of 'phantom' companies which attract investors with promises of very high interest rates, but whose directors soon abscond with their takings.[32] But even in the recognized banks depositors complain of officious clerks, obstructed access to withdrawals, unexplained levies on accounts and unreliable remittance and foreign-exchange service. At times Central Bank pressure has been exerted on banks to support insolvent state enterprises or to restrict withdrawals as a crude disinflationary instrument. In October the Central Bank reduced from 14 to two the banks authorized to deal in foreign exchange, alleging mismanagement in convertible currency dealing. In July 1996 it revoked the banking licence of Tver Universal Bank, one of the largest in the CIS, which had been active in exchanging Uzbek sum into roubles or dollars on the Almaty financial market; its disappearance caused difficulty to a number of CIS companies trading in Uzbekistan.[33]

Some of the divergence between policies advocated by the Central Bank and the National Bank for Foreign Economic Activities may be explained by the one being headed by an official from the Soviet period, Faizulla Mulajanov, while the other is led by a Western-trained economist, Rustam Azimov. In early October 1996 Mulajanov became concerned with the year's deterioration in the current-account balance (as described in Chapter 4): the current-account deficit of more than $2 billion equalled the gross foreign reserves. It was reportedly as a panic reaction to this that the Central Bank cancelled all permits to buy foreign currency, even for companies that had already made deposits in foreign-exchange accounts. In a reversion to Soviet-type preferences, the Bank announced that payments would be released on its own priority ranking, with imports of capital goods taking precedence over consumer goods. This intervention was contrary to the advice of many officials, the National Bank and international advisers. On 26 November the Resident Representative of the World Bank, Hasso Molineus, went public on the issue in an interview with Reuters, almost certainly in concert with the IMF which on 19 December cited the new controls as a factor in its suspension of credit disbursement. 'It is hard to understand', he said, 'why the Uzbek government should now introduce foreign-exchange and additional foreign-trade controls, and in fact move backwards from its stated objective of introducing current-account convertibility of the sum.'[34] That undertaking on liberalization had been given in 1994 as part of the country's agreement with the IMF and would have taken effect in 1997. Molineus dismissed the view that the foreign reserves were nearly exhausted: they were being replenished by an annual gold export of $800 million and by a bigger-than-forecast capital inflow. Reserves were

[32] *Central Asia Newsfile*, April 1996, p. 7 (giving a list of the authorized banks).
[33] *Central Asia Newsfile*, June 1996, p. 7.
[34] Reuters despatch by Shamil Baigin, 26 November 1996.

reported as sufficient for five months' imports and it was not restrictions on these that the situation required but a devaluation of the official exchange rate. The very slow fall during 1996 (36 sum to the dollar on 1 January to 40 in October, but dropping in November to 51.10) was much less than inflation, such that in real terms the sum had appreciated. Rumours of intended controls and frequent temporary shutdowns in foreign-currency payments pushed the unofficial rate up from barely 50 in August to 125–130 in late November. 'Shuttle traders' *(chelnoki)* were buying up consumer goods in Uzbekistan at the unofficial rate, while law-abiding retailers could not replenish their imported stock; foreign firms were selling their hard currency on the unofficial market but repatriating sum proceeds at the official rate.

In conditions where reserves were still adequate, devaluing the sum to a point between the official and the unofficial rates in order to defend it would be rational, and would reinstate the goal of convertibility in 1997. But this would renew inflation, contrary to the undertakings given to the IMF. The consumer price rise could, nevertheless, be modified by an across-the-board tariff cut and by greater stringency in government expenditure (notably in subsidies to enterprises); the banking sector should be strengthened by permitting the establishment of foreign banks (not just as representative offices or joint ventures).

3 CAPITAL AND TECHNOLOGICAL INFLOW

Foreign investment

In 1995 foreign direct investment (FDI) worldwide more than exceeded its previous peak to reach $318 billion, bringing the total invested to an estimated $2.7 trillion, or double that of 1988, and constituting 5.5 per cent of gross fixed capital in the host countries. The transition countries more than kept up with the worldwide rise, but remained a small share. In 1994 transition economies received 2.5 per cent ($5.9 billion out of $230 billion), but 3.8 per cent in 1995 ($12.2 billion). Within the CIS, Kazakstan – highly attractive to mining capital – has since independence been second only to Russia in accumulating FDI. At the beginning of 1996, the total stock in Kazakstan had reached $1,831 million, of which $723 million entered in 1995 alone. By contrast, the total stock of FDI in Uzbekistan was only $287 million, but with no less than $120 million entering during 1995;[1] the 1995 inflow was respectively 3.8 and 1.5 per cent of that year's GDP. For net transfers some allowance needs to be made for capital flight, since more than $60 billion has quit the CIS since 1992; the bulk, however, originated in Russia and Ukraine, and an estimate for cash held abroad by residents of Kazakstan is $2 billion.[2] Private funds that have left Central Asia are thought mostly to be derived from the drug traffic and illegal arms sales.

Excluding the OECD group to give a broad definition of the 'emerging markets' of the world, the share of transition countries in all private capital flows to emerging markets during 1990–95 was 13 per cent. Other capital inflows comprise official grants and loans. Such multilateral and bilateral support for systemic reform, together with privatization and the opening of stock exchanges, are behind the 15 per cent share of transition countries in total capital flow to non-OECD members ($1.64 trillion in 1990–95). Of official support, the IMF, as noted above, has so far provided $619 million to Kazakstan and $407 million to Uzbekistan, but the World Bank, the

---

[1] These estimates are from EBRD, *Transition Report 1996*, Table 8.5. Different, but provisional, estimates are in ECE, *East-West Investment News*, Summer 1996, p. 9. These, together with IMF, World Bank and UNCTAD documentation and a survey in the *Financial Times*, 27 September 1996, are sources for this section.

[2] Gregory Andrusz, 'Kazakstan', in Martin McCauley (ed.), *Investing in the Caspian Sea Region: Opportunity and Risk*, Cartermill, London, p. 33.

Asian Development Bank and the EBRD also are putting in substantial capital. Privatization and markets for the buying and selling of shares are less advanced in the two countries than in most transition states and it is predominantly through management contracts and joint ventures that private capital has entered. No less than 38 per cent of the 1995 increment of FDI into Kazakstan was due to management contracts – the government's favoured procedure in hydrocarbon extraction. Of the cumulative Kazak FDI stock at the start of 1996, 43 per cent was in that branch, with 37 per cent in tobacco, 10 per cent in metallurgy and only 2 per cent in other mining. Tobacco is also important in Uzbekistan, but mining has a major place through joint ventures in gold. In mid-1996 the distribution of the 2,397 such enterprises was 59 per cent in trade, hotels and catering, 27 per cent in mining and manufacturing and 7 per cent in other services.[3]

Cumulating inflows from 1989 to 1995, the EBRD estimates FDI at $110 per capita into Kazakstan, but only $13 per capita into Uzbekistan. The ranking reflects a business consensus until and including 1994. Large enterprises were offered for joint ventures and management contracts earlier in Kazakstan, where the general privatization programme also started sooner. Uzbekistan was not only later off those marks, but less prepared for an influx of foreigners. Thus, a correspondent observed in 1995: 'For almost two years investors have been flocking from Tashkent to Alma Ata because of frustration with the bureaucracy in Uzbekistan, where it can be difficult even to obtain a businessman's visa.'[4] During 1995, however, foreign business confidence in Kazakstan was eroded by several events. As described below, the unsavoury machinations on the Caspian Pipeline Consortium led Chevron to put its oil operations onto mere care and maintenance; there were scandals on tendering for joint ventures in Vasilovskoe gold and Chimkent refining. By contrast, in Uzbekistan the big BAT and Daewoo deals and the agreement with the IMF were raising confidence. The government has established a Foreign Investment Agency to facilitate inflow, but no corresponding body yet exists in Kazakstan. The publication in 1996 jointly by OECD and UNDP of a comprehensive *Investment Guide for Uzbekistan* must also have helped. FDI into Uzbekistan rose 41 per cent in 1995 over 1994 (the corresponding percentage was 14 in Kazakstan), but the sudden and arbitrary imposition of exchange control in Uzbekistan in late 1996 may have prejudiced this upswing.

More broadly, the EBRD finds a negative association between foreign investment and inflation, such that monetary weakness in the past has deterred foreign investors.[5] But investors would have realized that Uzbekistan's apparently better

[3] *Basic Results of Social and Economic Development in Uzbekistan,* January–June 1996.
[4] Steve Le Vine, *Financial Times,* 11 April 1995.
[5] EBRD, *Transition Report 1995,* Table 4.9.

record on this score (Table 2) was due to price control, rationing and compulsory state procurement, of which little now remains. A deterrent in both countries has been, as noted below, the gap between legislation and implementation and some arbitrariness in judicial and administrative relations with foreign companies. A boost was given to Kazakstan in October 1996 when it was ranked BB- both by IBCA (UK) and, in the next month, by Standard & Poor (US). Moody, the other US rating agency, has not yet released its assessment, and none of the three agencies has as yet given a rating for Uzbekistan. Both states have bilateral investment protection treaties with a number of Western states.

Western joint ventures

More than one-third of the world's FDI flow noted above is accounted for by inter-company transactions, a characteristic that underlines the value to a host economy of joint ventures.

To date the biggest Western capital commitment in Uzbekistan is the BAT purchase in 1994 of a 51 per cent share in the vertically integrated tobacco industry (down to 22 plantations in Urgut) for $60 million; an offer of a further 46 per cent for $54 million was deferred for five years. BAT plans to invest a further $232 million over five years in refurbishing the two cigarette factories. The project, competing in the Central Asian region with Philip Morris' similar purchase in Kazakstan, has its export dimension. A cigarette, 'Hon', blending local with imported tobaccos, was launched in March 1996 for both domestic and export sale; UzBAT's production was to be 14 billion cigarettes in 1996, but rebuilding the Samarkand plant will add 20 billion. As the law still does not allow private land ownership, BAT negotiated a 99-year lease for its factory sites at a predetermined rent. The South Korean firm Daewoo has joint ventures in motor vehicles ($100 million committed) in Andijan (production of cars and minibuses started in 1996), in unwoven fabrics in Tashlak (in 1996 it bought the latter completely – for $60 million – and expects the re-equipped firm to reach $25 million annual sales, of which some 90 per cent will be for export to other CIS states) and in television electronics (together $45 million). A joint venture with Germany's Mercedes Benz is making buses, while the French company Alcatel is re-equipping telecommunications (*The Economist*, 16 July 1994, wrote of the telephone system as 'falling to pieces ... Foreigners trying to work in Tashkent have been known to hire assistants merely to dial numbers'). Thomson is modernizing air traffic control, Biomed is in pharmaceuticals and there are other French ventures in non-financial services. The Turkish group Koç Holding is building a bus and trailer factory near Samarkand. The textiles sector, in particular, has attracted joint ventures: silk ribbons, with an Italian firm, in Namangan; cotton yarn and cloth, with a Korean firm in Toitepa, near Tashkent; and shirts and bed-linen, with a Turkish firm in Andijan. A Malaysian firm, Probadi, is redeveloping the Karaktai oil and gas deposit.

The official *Uzbekistan Business Guide* lists 116 offices of foreign firms (mostly in Tashkent, but also in Andijan, Namangan, Samarkand and Termez), but this figure had reached 166 by end-1995, including IBM (to serve also Azerbaijan, Tajikistan and Turkmenistan); sixty German firms (including Schering, Hoechst, Siemens and Deutsche Bank), and nearly twenty French firms (Louis Reihart, Olivier, Rhône-Poulenc and Delaplanque and others); and Japan (the Tomen Corporation). That gold-mining is at present a mainstay of the Uzbek economy is particularly due to a joint venture of which the foundations were laid (August 1991) just a month before independence, and which now commits Newmont of Denver, Colorado, to spending $225 million (of which $135 million is an EBRD loan). The Zarafshan joint venture (with the local Navoi Mining and Metallurgical Combine), which began by extracting gold from the tailings, is now a major open-cast operation, producing 55 tonnes in 1995, projected to 83 tonnes in 2000. Worried at pre-emption by other Central Asian governments, the EBRD, as co-financier, has insisted that the firm is not required to sell its output to the government for local currency. Lonrho, UK, took a joint venture with Navoi in 1995 in the Amantaytau gold mines, committing (with an IFC contribution) $100 million, and forecasting an output of 14.5 tonnes after four years. The Western Mining Corporation (Australia) and Mitsui Mindex (Japan) are negotiating for gold concessions, the latter also for tungsten.[6] Silver mining (open-cast, like the two big gold deposits), also in the Kyzyl Kum, has just begun. By 1 July 1996 a total of 2,397 joint ventures were operating – a rapid rise from the 1,395 at the beginning of 1995 – plus (on 1 January 1996) 144 foreign firms.

In Kazakstan major deals include Philip Morris investing $300 million in a cigarette factory, the Almaty Tobacco Combine, and associated tobacco plantations; and large ventures in the oil, gas and pipeline industries (as described below and in Chapter 4). On the other hand, Unilever was close to buying two margarine factories for $60 million, but could not obtain contracts for the supply of sunflower oil, and the sole facility in the former USSR producing vinyl fibres for the aerospace industry, Kustanaikhim Volokno, has found no buyer.

The Kazak government has been beset with problems in seeking joint ventures for its gold-mining (with reserves of 11 million troy ounces at Bakyrchik and 6.5 million ounces at Vasilovskoe). Bakyrchik Gold, with a 40 per cent share with the state mining firm, was floated on the London Stock Exchange in August 1993. After an initial and considerable rise in the price of its shares, it announced heavy losses and was res-

[6] Paper by B. Isakhodzaev and T. S. Shayabukov to an Adam Smith Institute Conference, Vienna, January 1996, pp. 4–5.

cued by Robert Friedland, a Canadian billionaire, in 1995. In December 1996 it became the first large gold mine in the CIS to be wholly foreign-owned. Bakyrchik Gold raised its stake to 85 per cent, and 15 per cent went to Indochina Goldfields (listed on the Toronto stock exchange), of which Friedland was chairman and owner of a 32 per cent stake. Meanwhile Friedland had declared that he was interested in Vasilovskoe, discovered in 1965, but only operating as a mine between 1988 and 1993, when losses forced its closure. After opening a tender in August 1994, sponsored by the EBRD, for a 50 per cent share with the Kazak state enterprise Altynalmas, Dominion Mining (Australia) spent several million dollars on a feasibility study, believing that it had secured exclusive rights. In December the government repudiated the discussions and allegedly used some of the company's confidential data to go to public tender. Then in April 1995 it cancelled the tender and handed the concession to Placer Dome (Canada), which involved itself in a sub-venture with a Russian businessman and President Nazarbayev's son-in-law. But that did not work out and Placer Dome has not yet received back its $35 million deposit. Western Mining, an earlier tenderer, and the huge RTZ-CRA (UK/Australia) declined to bid in a new round of tendering, but in July 1996 the government gave an option to Bakyrchik Gold, with Teck of Canada as lead company, together with First Dynasty, also controlled by Friedland, which has weighty Singapore investors and has moved its headquarters there. But the Teck-led consortium failed to reach agreement with the Kazak government by the August deadline: it seems that it offered terms (reportedly investment of $360 million, a bonus of $85 million and royalties for an 80 per cent share) which not all the consortium supported. In yet another surprise move, the government thereupon invited Lonrho to make an offer. Lonrho, which already has its Uzbek investment, has indicated that its terms, if any, would be less favourable than those mooted by Teck. Cogema (France) and World Wide Resources (Canada), also considering bids, have shown doubt over the government's cost projections.

The Kazak chrome industry (developed, as mentioned in Chapter 1, by prison labour in the Stalin period) experienced serious problems in 1995–6: the Russian electricity supply was cut for non-payment of bills and resumed only after settlement and a tripling of the electricity tariff. As world demand was slack at the time (mainly owing to an excess supply of stainless steel scrap), the new Kazkhrom (a corporatization in March 1996 of the mining and ferro-alloy enterprises) found itself in difficulty. In August 1996, however, a 55.2 per cent stake was purchased by the Japan Chromium Corporation, with 32.8 per cent retained by the state, 10 per cent held by staff and 2 per cent by domestic investment funds.[7] The new owner will invest $5 million in reconstruction.

[7] *Focus Central Asia*, No. 18, 30 September 1996, p. 14.

Foreign investment in Kazak hydrocarbons is defined by two characteristics: the vast potential, far exceeding local demand, of 2 billion tonnes of proved oil reserves, with as much again under Kazak-interest parts of the Caspian; and the need to evacuate exports through another CIS state (Russia, through which exports now run, Azerbaijan or Turkmenistan). Although access to the under-sea deposits remains in contention,[8] there is enough in the northwest territory to have already attracted the major transnational oil and gas corporations, as well as a score of minor ones. Operations are under way at 175 oilfields and 71 gasfields.[9] The Karachaganak gas deposits, with huge export potential, were initially developed under contract with the government by a consortium of British Gas and Agip, now joined by Texaco and Russia's Gazprom. At Tengiz on the Caspian littoral, the gas is for consumption within Kazakstan, but the 800 million tonnes of its 'super-giant' oil reserves are to be exploited for sale in Europe. Chevron was the first to sign up with the government in Tengizchevroil; Mobil subsequently purchased part of the government share. Since the only existing evacuation route is Transneft's network into Russia and numerous difficulties (as well as the war in Chechenia) arose in accessing it, a crucial issue is of evacuation, discussed in Chapter 4 in the context of international transport. Other blocks of the Tengiz deposit have been promised to a consortium of seven majors (Agip, British Gas, Mobil, Total, Shell, BP and Statoil). Other major oil corporations bidding for Kazak oil are Exxon and Texaco (Atyubinsk) and Amoco (south of Tengiz).[10]

A complex situation has arisen with respect to the Chimkent oil refinery, which is the terminus of a crude supply piped from the West Siberian Yuzhneftegaz. In 1995 Yuzhneftegaz, the Chimkent refinery and several other companies were integrated into a state-owned YuTEK (a Russian acronym for Southern Fuel Energy Company), envisaging a joint venture with LUKoil to exploit the Kumkol deposits (with 42 million tonnes of reserves) in Kazakhstan; Kumkol lies northeast of the Aral Sea, has some gas and adjoins the Pridorozh gasfield. However, at a privatization auction in June 1996 the US company Samson International won 89.5 per cent of Yuzhneftegaz and Vitol Beheer BV, a Netherlands company with Swiss capital,

---

[8] See John Roberts, *Caspian Pipelines*, FSS Key Paper, RIIA, London, 1996, pp. 49–53, and Allison (ed.), *Challenges for the Former Soviet South*, Part 5 by Kaser and Mehrotra, 'The Central Asian Economies after Independence', pp. 301–2, and Part 6 by Gavan McDonell, 'The Euro-Asian Corridor', pp. 344–8.

[9] From a map of oil- and gasfields and pipelines (existing, under construction or planned) and of coal deposits in Central Asia, the Caucasus and Northwest China, published by the *Petroleum Economist* and Ernst and Young, from the latter's offices in London, Houston, Moscow, Almaty and Baku (3rd edn, 1996).

[10] *Financial Times*, 11 July 1996, Supplement on Kazakhstan, p. vi.

gained Chimkent.[11] But under the Kazak privatization law, the auction winner gains only the right to negotiate development terms and investment, and Samson had to seek permission for the Kumkol-LUKoil venture. This was refused and Samson was divested at the end of July; the Committee for the Management of State Property declared the winner of Yuzhneftegaz to be Hurricane Kumkol, a subsidiary of Hurricane Hydrocarbons of Canada. The incident was an example of untoward practice, which lowered the Western business estimation of the Kazak authorities.

Joint ventures in other branches include a Korean half-share (the Samsung Corporation) in the Zhezkazgan Copper Combine (to produce 200,000 tonnes by the year 2000); and the RJR Nabisco (US) purchase of the Chimkent Confectionery Factory.[12] Some small joint ventures are in services (Alexander Howden Reinsurance Brokers of London and the state-owned Kazakinstrakh are pooling convertible currency business with the country), and the EBRD is participating in a number of infrastructure projects, of which the biggest is reconstruction of the Caspian port of Aktau.

Involvement of Russian firms

There is an argument that some Russian policy-makers have an 'ultimate objective to compel Central Asian reintegration with Russia on Moscow's terms, mainly by using economic levers'.[13] The economic history of the former USSR renders close economic relationships inevitable, and, as just discussed, those relations are especially promoted in the field of energy: the participation of major Russian companies (state, semi-state and private) is a significant feature of Kazak hydrocarbon exploitation and evacuation. For Kazakstan the break-up of the USSR transformed many long-standing contractual links into a transnational status. This was particularly true of mineral-processing industries of the Urals, the Kuzbas and northern Kazakhstan. One more distant link between the Erdenet mines in Mongolia was of enriched copper, molybdenum and gold ores through Russia for processing in Kazakhstan at Balkhash, and which is now in jeopardy by reason of the latter's bankruptcy.

[11] According to *Russia Express: Reporting the Republics of the Former Soviet Union*, No. 183 (28 October 1996), p. 11, at $60 million and further investment guaranteed of $230 million for facilities which could, according to the source, be worth anything between $75 million and $380 million. Coal is to substitute for some of the feedstock to replace imports from Russia.
[12] From 1988 this firm joined with Chevron and other US companies (notably Ford and Mercator) to negotiate a set of barter deals whereby the profits from the US side's investments would be converted into dollars from the proceeds of oil sales.
[13] Stephen Blank, 'Energy, Economics and Security in Central Asia: Russia and Its Rivals', *Central Asian Survey*, Vol. 14, No. 3, 1995, pp. 373–406.

A number of 'financial-industrial groups' based in Russia have extended to enterprises in Kazakstan.[14] Among those already formed are 'Ural'skie zavody' in heavy engineering, telecommunications and defence engineering; 'Interros' in ferrous metallurgy; and 'Altai' in non-ferrous metals; negotiations are in progress in titanium-magnesium between mining enterprises in East Kazakstan *oblast* and two Russian metallurgical plants.[15] A Russian-Uzbek insurance firm, Metropolis, is among the few linkages made with firms in Uzbekistan. During the CIS Summit in October 1996, Russia and Kazakstan signed a double taxation agreement.

Investment incentives

A Presidential Decree of January 1996 in Kazakstan authorized the establishment of free trade zones, in which no customs duties are levied and investors gain substantial tax benefits. Only one zone, created under Soviet law, has as yet been established – the small town of Lisakovsk with a mere 11,100 total employment.[16] There are already four such zones in Kyrgyzstan, but Uzbekistan has not yet taken this step.

The Kazak Foreign Investment Law which took effect in January 1995 assures foreign investors no less favourable treatment than is accorded to domestic investors, assures legal validity to contracts for ten years, even if the law should be changed in that period, protects foreigners against expropriation (save on national security grounds, which would evoke proper compensation) and against constraint on the repatriation of profits. Hydrocarbon extraction is subject to the government's right of pre-emption, but at world market prices, and in an emergency its right to requisitioning, but again with due compensation.[17] Uzbek legislation of June 1991, amended in July 1992, was considerably improved in May 1994, when the foreign share of equity required in the Uzbek entity was lowered from 30 to 10 per cent; the legislation also stipulated that foreign investors cannot be legally in a worse position than domestic ones, and safeguarded them against nationalization. Imports for their own use and exports from their production may not be subject to quota or licence. Certain joint ventures and foreign enterprises are taxed at lower rates than purely domestic firms (confirmed by the revised tax law of December 1995) and from June 1996 are exempt from corporation and land taxes and VAT for an initial two years.

[14] On their establishment in Russia, see Irina Starodubrovskaya, 'Financial-Industrial Groups: Illusions and Reality'; and Lev Freinkman, 'Financial-Industrial Groups in Russia: Emergence of Large Diversified Private Companies', *Communist Economies and Economic Transformation*, Vol. 7, No. 1, March 1995, pp. 5–19 and 51–66.
[15] E. M. Ivanov, 'Kazakstan, Russia and Prospects for Economic Union within the CIS', in Kozhokin (ed.), *Kazakhstan..*, pp. 45–58.
[16] *Kazakstan Human Development Report 1996*, p. 28.
[17] CBI, *Doing Business in Kazakstan*, pp. 64–5.

By comparison with other CIS members, the two republics have a very low incidence of crimes against foreigners. Russian 'contract killings', very few of which are brought to trial, and the assassination in Moscow in November 1996 of a US businessman (whose ownership of 40 per cent of a hotel joint venture was under arbitration) provoked reflections on 'physical hazard, coupled with political uncertainty and a stifling tax system' which kept annual foreign investment in Russia equal to about a fortnight's inflow into China.[18] The powerful central and regional hierarchs of Kazakstan and Uzbekistan, noted in Chapter 1, are assured of sufficient policing and by and large favour foreign investors. Such investors, as in many post-communist states and elsewhere in the Orient, need to take account of conditions conducive to bribery, corruption, cronyism and nepotism.

The physical security of installations and equipment has as yet not been jeopardized. The internal danger in both countries could be of xenophobic or Islamic fundamentalist origin or incidental to civil unrest. Strong political authority offers a guarantee at present, but it should not be taken for granted. Several thousand trade unionists and others demonstrated in Almaty and other towns in Kazakstan in October 1996 in protest against unpaid wages and pensions and irregular ('wild') privatization. The problem is rather of safe transit to and from the two landlocked states, such as pilfering from railway wagons across Russia, very long road-haulage times across Turkey, Iran and Turkmenistan, and the interruption of routes by war in Afghanistan, Tajikistan and Azerbaijan (including the Trans-Caspian rail and lorry ferry). Long-distance oil and gas export pipelines may now be safer if the Chechen settlement holds, but western Asia is rife with actual and potential terrorism and irredentism.

More prominent in the minds of foreign investors is a general penetration of inefficiency and corruption among officialdom and difficulty caused by the hiatus between legislation and actual implementation. Arbitrary action in the public sector and underhand and criminal practice in the private sector feature in many transition states and in Asian market economies (and elsewhere), but are no less a deterrent to Western business entry in Kazakstan and Uzbekistan. In April 1996 the Prime Minister of Kazakstan, Akezhan Kazhegeldin, requested the Almaty Office of the International Tax and Investment Center of Washington, DC to survey foreign firms in the country on their perception of investment constraints. Volatile laws and regulations, lack of consistency between and within ministries, and a 'very adversarial' attitude of officials towards foreign business were particularly observed.[19]

---

[18] *The Economist*, 9 November 1996; it noted 560 such assassinations in 1995 and 450 in ten months of 1996 (with respectively only 60 and 10 assassins found).
[19] *Kazakstan Survey*, June 1996, p. 6.

Domestic investment

Foreign investment is all the more important because little capital equipment is being installed in the home private sector. Uzbekistan and Kyrgyzstan were the only CIS members to exhibit an increase in capital investment in 1995: 82,200 million sum from all sources of finance was 2 per cent above 1994, which, however, had been 22 per cent below 1993. Kazakstan investment, also from all sources, was 107.7 billion tenge, or 27 per cent below 1994, which in turn had been 15 per cent below 1993.[20] An extreme view is that, apart from Uzbekistan, the Central Asian states depend for their investment on Russia and that little capital transfer is to be expected from that country.[21]

Although Central Asia was not part of the relevant IMF database, the region reflects the trend among transition economies to show a lower propensity to save – for countries less advanced in transition the share of domestic savings in GDP dropped from 27 to 15 per cent of GDP between 1989 and 1995.[22] As noted above, banks have as yet not fully served the function of mobilizing savings. On their use of funds, a recent analysis of the Uzbek record points to the dominance of house-building in domestic construction and the scant installation of new machinery and technology other than in foreign firms, as well as the inadequacy of the banks to mobilize domestic savings. Only about 5 per cent of bank credits is long-term, most being one to three months' trade lending.[23] Legal compulsion in Uzbekistan to trans-act only in sum, in conjunction with exchange control and inflation, leads house-holds and small business to hoard foreign currency (mostly dollars) and hence to sterilize investible funds; capital flight, similarly motivated, further depletes home capital formation. In autumn 1996 a Presidential Decree, 'On Measures for Controlling Circulation of Foreign Currency', required foreign firms and embassies and international organizations to pay Uzbek employees solely in sum and limited the export of foreign currency by residents to $500; imposition of a 2 per cent tax on bringing in more than $5,000 per person will also deter the repatriation of funds already held abroad.[24]

[20] CIS Statistical Committee, *Statistichesky Byulleten'*, January 1996, p. 49.
[21] Stanislav Zhukov, 'Economic Development in the States of Central Asia', in Boris Rumer (ed.), *Central Asia in Transition: Dilemmas of Political and Economic Development*, M.E. Sharpe, Armonk NY and London, p. 112.
[22] *World Development Report 1996*, p. 80.
[23] David Dyker, 'Investment Trends and Prospects in Uzbekistan', *Central Asia Newsfile*, August–September 1996, pp. 10–19.
[24] *Focus Central Asia*, November 1996, p. 62.

4 EXTERNAL ECONOMIC RELATIONS

The definition of trade

Kazak and Uzbek statistics, like Russian, distinguish trade with the 'near' and 'far' abroad, the distinction being the former Soviet frontiers; the IMF usage, respectively 'traditional' and 'non-traditional', is free of politico-geographical identification, but the UN ECE practice of distinguishing 'CIS states' from 'other countries' is more apposite because it relates to an actual economic grouping. The Soviet central planning mechanism made both states substantially dependent on exchanges with the rest of the USSR, the 'traditional' partners. The role of non-ferrous metals and cotton as national import substitutes during Stalin's autarkic five-year plans compelled the southern regions of the two republics to be fed on Siberian wheat and dairy produce and to grow cotton instead of foodstuffs. The expansion in Kazakstan, and the establishment in Uzbekistan of steel and engineering during the Second World War increased the republics' trade dependency on Russia and Ukraine and to a lesser degree on the other Union Republics. Trade statistics in the Soviet period ignored 'shuttle trade' effected by travellers between the Union Republics, even though much of the vegetables, dairy produce and flowers was brought to markets in Russia from the republics to the south (the State Bank made regional estimates of such sales as part of its monthly 'cash plans').

Such personal traffic has expanded since independence as travel restrictions for citizens have been relaxed and include many foreign countries. China, India and Turkey are the source of much of this 'shuttle trade': the Kazak aircraft destroyed in the mid-air collision with a Saudi plane near Delhi in November 1996 had been chartered for a shopping spree in India. The trade returns generally cited are those registered by the customs authorities, but for Kazakstan the Statistical Committee and the National Bank are now compiling unrecorded trade, of which imports greatly exceed exports.[1] Both republics nevertheless remain strongly trade-linked to the other CIS transition economies, especially the three Slav republics, on whose growth they are hence partly dependent. It is all too obvious to point out that the central planning mechanism tied both Union Republics to exchanges with the rest of the

---

[1] *Kazakstan Economic Trends*, Second Quarter 1996, p. 115.

USSR. The role of cotton (in Uzbekistan and south Kazakstan, as also in Tajikistan and Turkmenistan) as a national import substitute during Stalin's planned autarky had been facilitated by the construction of the Turk-Sib Railway, linking Almaty and Tashkent with Novosibirsk and completed in 1930, which allowed Central Asia to be fed on Siberian wheat and dairy produce and to grow cotton instead of foodstuffs. The construction of two Trans-Kazakstan railways after the Second World War[2] fostered the expansion of minerals exports, while the establishment of a steel and engineering industry required imports of metals, semi-fabricates and components.

The direction of trade

In Soviet times the Union Republican Planning Committees (Gosplans) did not have to concern themselves with trade and payments balances. Settlements (which in any event were not at market-clearing prices) were not effected on a republican basis and transfers were made from the All-Union budget when – as was usual – republican revenue did not cover republican expenditure. At the end of that period, Kazakstan had the largest inter-republican trade deficit of any Union Republic (12 per cent of GDP), whereas Uzbekistan had an export surplus (2 per cent of GDP). At independence the transfers from Moscow were stopped and management of the trade balance became the responsibility of the new governments. At the same time, it was in the countries' interest to shift the direction of trade, preferably to nearby states in which they had a competitive advantage and to partners with convertible currencies. By 1995 just over half of Kazak exports and two-thirds of imports were to and from other CIS states, but for Uzbekistan that year marked a shift from a CIS majority to a minority in both exports and imports.[3]

Of Kazakstan's $4,990 million exports in 1995, $2,817 million (56 per cent) went to the 'near abroad', of which $2,813 million went to Russia, $160 million to Uzbekistan and $121 million to Ukraine. The European Union took $1,082 (of which $523 million was recorded to the Netherlands, $170 million to Germany and $98 to the UK); among other substantial buyers of Kazak goods were China ($304 million), Turkey ($71 million) and the United States ($49 million).

The corresponding 1995 returns for Uzbekistan also put Russia as the largest partner – $902 million exports (26 per cent) and 1,057 million imports (28 per cent), followed by Kazakstan – $271.5 exports (8 per cent) and $303 million imports (8 per cent). Among other CIS members, exports that year exceeded $100 million only

---

[2] Extending the Karaganda/Balkhash line from Moyynty to Chu and connecting the western Uzbek line to Astrakhan.

[3] Summary returns are in ECE, *East-West Investment News*, Autumn 1996, p. 24.

to neighbouring Tajikistan and Turkmenistan, with imports exceeding that value only from Ukraine. Europe figured among 'non-traditional' partners with just $118 million of exports (3 per cent) and $194 million of imports (5 per cent).

In contrast to its heavy import deficit with the CIS in 1994, Kazakstan achieved an almost precise equilibrium of trade with that group in 1995, by increasing exports. Uzbekistan, also gained an exact balance of trade in 1995, and slashed its CIS export surplus of 1994 by cutting both exports and imports, through a decimation (literally to one-tenth of the 1994 level) of energy imports and a one-third cut in purchases of food and other agricultural produce (as part of the drive to self-sufficiency in grain). The country also switched a deficit with 'non-traditional' partners in 1994 to a surplus in 1995 by effecting a large rise in exports and a smaller rise in imports.

Uzbekistan is among the world's five largest producers of cotton (its ginned output of 1,656,000 tonnes was 9.5 per cent of the world crop in 1989), and the second biggest cotton exporter (after the United States), supplying one-fifth of world exports (1,483,000 tonnes ginned weight or 21.8 per cent in 1989).[4] In 1992 cotton earned 77 per cent of the country's earnings outside the former USSR, but a combination of declining cotton sales and a small rise in mineral sales reduced the share to 65 per cent in 1993 and 50 per cent in 1995. When captive users were the Soviet norm, the quality of cotton delivered was generally below world standards, but by and large these have now been met. That record of poor quality was among the reasons why Russian buyers, once freed from a single supplier, tapered off purchases from Uzbekistan: in 1995 Russia bought from Uzbekistan only one-third of the amount it had bought in 1993 and since 1996 has largely switched from Uzbekistan in favour of Western suppliers. Another cause of diminishing purchases was the collapse of Russian textile production (19 per cent of the 1990 level in 1995), and a further factor was the imposition in May 1996 by the Russian Duma of a 20 per cent VAT on CIS cotton imports; these had previously been free of tax, but were now on a par with imports from the 'non-traditional' partners.[5] The UK and both Kazak and Uzbek trade returns disagree on mutual trade. UK trade returns for 1994 and 1995 (Table 5) show an import deficit with Kazakstan and an export surplus with Uzbekistan. But Kazakstan's returns show balanced trade in 1994 and a much bigger margin in its favour for 1995; Uzbek returns show balances the reverse of the British, apparently because the latter records cotton bought by British firms (of which A. Meredith Jones and Co. is the largest dealer[6]) as sold to the UK, whereas many of the shipments go to other countries, including Russia.

---

[4] For a study of cotton production and trade, see IMF Economic Reviews, No. 4, 1994, *Uzbekistan*, IMF, Washington, DC, pp. 92–4.

[5] An account is in *Segodnya* (Moscow), 13 April and 16 May 1996.

[6] The firm (which also has a joint farming venture in the Fergana Valley) sells one-tenth of Uzbek cotton exports (*The Times*, 19 January 1996, advertising supplement on Uzbekistan).

Table 5: UK trade with Kazakstan and Uzbekistan (£ million at current prices)

	Kazakstan		Uzbekistan	
	1994	1995	1994	1995
UK imports	70.6	48.9	3.5	1.6
UK exports	40.7	26.6	17.3	15.1
Visible balance	-29.9	-22.3	+13.8	+13.5
Import rank in UK trade	78	88	152	164
Export rank in UK trade	99	110	126	135

Source: Statistics Directorate, Department of Trade and Industry.

The external account

The Kazak Action Programme for the Deepening of Reforms 1996–8, which followed a similar programme for 1994–5, laid special emphasis on the encouragement of investment: in 1995 foreign direct investment had amounted to some $723 million. Against this Kazakstan continues to run a current-account deficit, of about $800 million over 1994–6. But in 1995 the visible balance had swung positive. Kazakstan's exports (as recorded by customs statistics) had increased from $3,231 million in 1994 to $4,990 million in 1995 and were forecast at $6 billion in 1996.[7] This offset rising imports to shrink the visible deficit (recorded and unrecorded trade) from $923 million in 1994 to $223 million in 1995 and swing to a surplus in the first quarter of 1996 ($668 million). Rising unit-values, which may prove temporary, played a big part in the export gains, but it is possible now to see Kazakstan as moving ahead on foreign investment and export-led growth.

Total Uzbek exports had exceeded imports in 1994 and 1995 and the surplus had more than offset the deficit on invisibles in 1994 and most of the invisibles deficit in 1995. Thus the current-account balance had been +$118 million in 1994 and -$53 million in 1995. The capital account was by and large equilibrated in those two years. But the overvaluation of the sum has been encouraging imports and deterring exports, and official forecasts for 1996 showed exports unchanged from the 1995 level ($3,805 million) while imports would be some $4,000 million against $3,589 million in 1995; add in the growing invisibles deficit, and a current-account deficit of about $620 million was shown. This was the apparent foreign-exchange crisis which led to the sudden restriction of transactions as described in Chapter 2. Foreign

---

[7] *Kazakstan Economic Trends*, Second Quarter 1996, pp. 17 and 22. Unrecorded exports seem to have been only $140 million, but unrecorded imports are large.

investment has, however, been flowing (some $750 million net inflow was foreseen) and the capital surplus would have been close to offsetting the current-account deficit. In the event the full-year outturn based on nine months' returns showed lower exports (especially for convertible currency – down by nearly a billion dollars) and imports likely to exceed $5 billion.

According to the Bank for International Settlements,[8] at end-June 1995 Kazak and Uzbek entities and residents had bank deposits respectively of $419 and $997 million in BIS reporting banks. But after deducting banks' loans, only Uzbeks were in net credit ($659 million), while Kazaks were in debt ($362 million).

In July 1996 Kazakstan signed Article VII of the IMF Agreement, committing itself to refrain from restricting current-account transactions or from implementing discriminatory currency arrangements.[9] The tenge is hence convertible on current account and floats. Building on that basis, the Kazak Securities Commission promoted in London the country's first bond issue in December 1996, explaining that although 'the country did not urgently need the funds ... our objective is to establish a track record and open the international capital markets for Kazak borrowers'; ABN Amro Hoare Govett was the lead manager when the $200 million bond was successfully floated on 9 December 1996.[10] Uzbekistan, on the other hand, had during 1996 sharply reduced the value of foreign currency offered for auction by the Central Bank, and the rules on converting the sum into foreign exchange (including for profit repatriation) were non-transparent.[11] The imposition in November 1996 of the arbitrary limitations described in Chapter 2 were thus the culmination of a process of deliberalization; as stated earlier, the margin between the grossly over-valued official rate and the unofficial rate was by late 1996 very wide. Uzbekistan has so far decided against launching a bond issue in the international financial markets.

Multilateral links within the CIS

As members of the CIS, both Kazakstan and Uzbekistan not only commit around half their trade to the group, but participate in the numerous discussions of that organization; of the two, Uzbekistan undertakes fewer commitments.[12] The principal economic discussions take place in the Interstate Economic Committee, estab-

---

[8] *International Banking and Financial Market Developments,* November 1996, p. 16.
[9] *IMF Survey,* 12 August 1996.
[10] *Financial Times,* 3 and 10 December 1996.
[11] Summary of exchange-rate regimes from EBRD, *Transition Report 1996,* pp. 156, 184.
[12] See Mark Webber, *CIS Integration Trends: Russia and the Former Soviet South,* FSS Key Paper, RIIA, January 1997.

lished in October 1994, and the Interstate Monetary Committee (May 1995):[13] they have been discussing modalities of implementing the Treaty on the Establishment of a Payments Union (September 1993), but to date negotiations have been limited to bilateral dealings. A CIS Economic Court serves as arbitrator between economic entities in transnational disputes.[14] In the wake of an abrupt and disorderly scission of intra-Soviet exchanges, more limited technical agreements are nevertheless of mutual value in improving normalized relationships. Examples in 1996 were the CIS Committee on Standardization, Metrology and Certification (April, Ashgabat), which was concerned with harmonization and regulation of quality control and certification; and the Fourth Conference of CIS Bankers (May, Yalta) seeking to regularize financial and currency markets. A CIS Committee for the Defence Industries has re-established collaboration among enterprises which were among the most seriously disrupted by the liquidation of the Warsaw Treaty Organization and the all-round military budget cuts that followed the end of the Cold War. It is also a forum for the *matériel* aspects of the transactions of the Council of CIS Defence Ministers. The latter met in Dushanbe in October 1996, without Turkmenistan and Uzbekistan, but both Kazakstan's and Uzbekistan's presidents attended a summit with Russia, Kyrgyzstan and Tajikistan earlier that month to warn the Afghan Taliban that any incursion into CIS territory would be firmly resisted. A full CIS presidential summit had taken place in May in Moscow. The CIS Interparliamentary Assembly provides another dimension to discussion, focusing at its May meeting in Bishkek on the concordance of laws.

The five Turkic CIS states have established with Turkey what Turkish President Süleyman Demirel called (at a summit meeting in Istanbul in October 1994) 'not a zone of influence but a zone of cooperation'; they participate in the Organization of the Islamic Conference (OIC).[15] Reference is sometimes made to the idea of a united 'Turkestan – Our Common Home', and other thoughts of reviving past ideals of pan-Turkic or pan-Turanian unity have been expressed, but none of the governments wish others to have hegemony.[16] Their practical focus is on trade and on transport infrastructure: a Partnership Agreement, approved by the five presidents in March 1992, led to the establishment of an Economic Council of the five

[13] Abraham Becker, 'Russia and Economic Integration in the CIS', *Survival*, Vol. 38, No. 4, Winter 1996–7, pp. 117–36, points out that its powers are formally supranational.

[14] V. Tsybukov, *Problemy pravopreyemstva v SNG*, Moscow, MGIMO, 1994, documents the legal instruments then valid among the CIS membership.

[15] The *Journal of Islamic Studies,* Vol. 7, No. 2, July 1996, is devoted to the theme of Islam in Central Asia and the Caucasus.

[16] See Heribert Dieter, 'Regional Integration in Central Asia: Current Economic Position and Prospects, *Central Asian Survey,* Vol. 15, No. 3/4, esp. pp. 378–84; Boris Rumer (ed.), *Central Asia in Transition: Dilemmas of Political and Economic Development,* esp. pp. 17–55.

in January 1993.[17] President Niyazov's determination to be in sole control of Turkmenistan cuts that country out of most transnational cooperation, and Uzbekistan did not adhere to the 'Economic and Humanitarian Integration' signed in March 1996 between Russia, Belarus, Kazakstan and Kyrgyzstan (otherwise, the 'Four' or the Quadrilateral); it was declared open not only to CIS members but to others, for whom variant forms of integration could be found. At the ensuing trilateral meeting of the presidents of Kazakstan, Kyrgyzstan and Uzbekistan, Karimov declared his preference for agreements within the CIS as a whole, but that integration among the 'Four' was not an obstacle to appropriate Uzbek integration with them. The 'Four' established an Integration Committee (May 1996, Moscow) with a programme of coordination in economic reform, monopoly regulation and a unified electric power system which would join Uzbekistan, already in the Central Asian grid, to the Russian Unified Energy System. When Turkmenistan links with Iran's grid (a cable is now being installed from Nebit-Dag to Mazandaran), it expects to be able to supply power to Uzbekistan.

Trilateral integration

In 1994, Kazakstan, Kyrgyzstan and Uzbekistan signed a trilateral agreement on a united economic zone which established committees including an Intergovernmental Council, a Council of Prime Ministers and an Executive Committee and founded a jointly-owned Central Asian Bank for Cooperation and Development. Very little happened in the first two years – tariffs persisted, excise duties varied and the national currencies were not freely convertible with one another. The three presidents met in Bishkek in May 1996 to give the cooperation an ambitious impetus: proposals included harmonization of import and export tariffs, and of competition legislation; and the reduction of legal and economic obstacles to the movement of labour and capital. The three Central Banks were required to develop a trilateral payments mechanism for settlements in both national and convertible currencies; and the Executive Committee was asked to formulate a scheme for free economic zones in the border territories of Kazakstan, Kyrgyzstan and Uzbekistan (as noted above, Kazakstan has one, and Kyrgyzstan four such zones), and a programme of economic cooperation to the year 2000. The Prime Ministers' Council in April 1996 took decisions on a common transport policy, on the utilization of Central Asian gas pipelines and on intergovernmental land rental, and formed an Industrial-Financial Group for the electronics industry (Tsentrazelektron).

[17] It was at this meeting that the five presidents decided to change from the Soviet usage 'Srednyaya Aziya' (which excluded Kazakstan) to the comprehensive 'Tsentral'naya Aziya' ('A New Turkestan', *Nezavisimaya gazeta*, 3 February 1993).

Russia and Tajikistan were granted observer status in the trilateral union at a summit conference in Almaty in August 1996, which also approved a programme for a single economic area of the three republics with effect from 1998, and the setting up of special economic zones in border areas to encourage cross-frontier trade. The Central Asian Bank for Cooperation and Development is reported to have already made some fruitful loans: the Kyrgyz Electromechanical Plant was able to increase output (including delivery of small electric motors to Kazakstan and Uzbekistan) by 30 per cent in 1995, helped by a Bank credit, and in April 1996 the big Tashkent Textiles Factory sought a loan from it to upgrade its cotton thread production, so as to replace supplies from St Petersburg which knitwear plants in the three states currently use. With its head office in Almaty, the Bank has furnished a number of smaller loans to firms in Kazakstan. The August 1996 Summit agreed that each of the three states would contribute a further $1 million to its capital.[18]

Tariffs and quantitative restrictions

When the two states join the World Trade Organization they will have to negotiate the customs-union or free-trade relationships with other Central Asian or CIS states, adopt the standard most-favoured-nation (MFN) and reciprocity arrangements and be subject to WTO disputes procedure. Tariffs and quotas are currently imposed by both states, new structures being adopted by Kazakstan on 15 August 1995 and by Uzbekistan on 1 October 1995, each tightening import and relaxing export constraints. Kazakstan, in accordance with its commitments to the 'Four', adopted the Russian System of Preferences. It also enumerated a list of 'strategically important resources' which could be exported only with specific permission, and introduced the Russian procedure of 'passports' to record shipment and payment details of each transaction as a means of inhibiting further capital flight.[19] On 1 July 1996 all export taxes except that on grain were repealed. Uzbekistan effected two groups of import changes – a number of tariff exemptions (introduced in January 1994) were withdrawn and certain high protective barriers were applied. Thus – in pursuance of an undertaking to the joint motor-vehicle venture, UzDaewoo – the import duty on cars was raised to 100 per cent; a protective 50 per cent duty was imposed on carpets. Export quotas were cut to three major product groups (ferrous metals, hydrocarbons and cotton), but there was political motivation in the prohibition from import of all newspapers, manuscripts and film. The abrupt imposition of payments restrictions in November 1996 reversed, doubtless temporarily, the liberalizing trend.

[18] BBC, *Inside Central Asia*, Issue 135, 19–25 August 1996.
[19] Zhaniya Usenova and Scott Horton, 'New Customs Union Leads Kazakstan to Liberalize Import/Export Constraints', *Central Asian Monitor*, No. 4, 1996, pp. 30–36, describe the country's preceding and current tariffs and quantitative restrictions on trade and on payments.

Collaboration in water conservation

The hydrography of the two republics differs. Precipitation in the steppe and semi-steppe zones varies from year to year, but is mostly adequate for grain crops; and in both the north and the west the territory is crossed by large rivers – the Ural, the Tobol, the Ishim and the Irtysh. There are three large lakes in the arid zones, but in that southern part Kazakstan shares the Syr Darya River with Uzbekistan. Uzbekistan's hot and dry climate – Termez has the warmest mean temperature of the CIS (32°C average in July) – renders essential the 52 cubic km of water that its rivers annually supply. Irrigated agriculture uses an average of 44 cu. km, industry 6 cu. km and households 2 cu. km. Loss through leakage and evaporation is high (two-fifths of Amu Darya water leaks away in arterial channels, and more goes in field channels under farm control), and substantial investment is required in lining the many canals. The shrinkage of the Aral Sea (its 1995 area was half that of 1960), owing to the excessive extraction from the inflowing Syr Darya and Amu Darya rivers, has become a crucial issue at both the regional and the international level.

The presidents of Kazakstan, Kyrgyzstan, Tajikistan, Turkmenistan and Uzbekistan met in March 1995 to seek solutions to this, the region's greatest ecological problem, and, following a report on the Aral Sea by the World Bank (which furnished a $32 million loan for conservation works), a UNESCO symposium (Tashkent, September 1995) heard a suggestion by the Uzbek First Deputy Minister for Land Melioration and Water Conservation, Abdurakhim Zhalalov, for reviving the Soviet scheme (first mooted in 1951, abandoned in 1986) to divert some the northward flow of the Ob' and Irtysh to replenish the Aral Sea; but the capital cost of $115 billion that he put on it and the uncertainty of environmental effects ruled it out.

A crucial issue is payment for water (which was briefly levied in the late 1950s and 1960s), for its absence encourages waste and requires heavy unrequited outlay by the government utilities and virtually arbitrary quantity rationing. A recent study has found three factors inhibiting change:

(1) Few administrators of water authorities have changed since economic change began; despite occasional exposure to Western consultants and seminars, 'new ideas, in particular to the principles of water pricing ... have not yet had any significant effect on practice'.
(2) Western precedents on international water allocation are themselves poor guides.
(3) Cotton plantation managements oppose water pricing, and Central Asian governments are still minded to subsidize them (or invest on their behalf) rather than confront them or prejudice the revenue from export sales of cotton.[20]

---

[20] Bryan Roberts, Barents-KPMG and University of Miami, 'Central Asian Water Allocation: Change through Crisis', *Central Asia Newsfile*, April 1996, pp. 8–9.

An issue between Uzbekistan and Kyrgyzstan is that Syr Darya water originates in the latter's territory and is held in reservoirs close to the Uzbek border, of which Toktogul (1.2 MW) on the Naryn is the largest. In Soviet times the primordial ranking of cotton production led to release of the spring/early summer accumulation of water to irrigate the growing cotton in the Fergana Valley and further in Uzbekistan during the summer, whereas the economic interest of Kyrgyzstan, with its fossil-energy deficit, was to retain the water until autumn/winter to feed its hydroelectric plants during the peak demand seasons for electricity demand (the mean January temperature is -1.3°C in Tashkent, but -6.6°C in Bishkek). Low winter precipitation made it evident that 1995 would be a low-water year and the two governments agreed that Kyrgyzstan would release the water demanded by Uzbekistan and supply summertime electricity (hydropower is of course a byproduct of the water release) for cotton against Uzbek natural gas and gas-fired electricity in the winter. Kazakstan, which benefits from the Syr Darya water further downstream, joined the negotiations, but declined the contract, complaining that 'water should not be for sale'.[21] The trilateral meeting of the Presidents of Kazakstan, Kyrgyzstan and Uzbekistan in May 1996 reached a new agreement on the regulation of these jointly shared water resources and hydropower.

This agreement – if it holds – seems to have been complemented by agreement between Presidents Karimov and Saparmurat Niyazov (Turkmenbashi) of Turkmenistan in January 1996 on water flow along the Amu Darya; they symbolically met at Chardzou, a border town on that river, and just 80 km from the disputed Kokdumalak hydrocarbons (as noted below, p. 63).

Bilateral economic relations

The breakdown of the command economy, the disappearance of a single currency and the erection of tariff and other barriers to trade left many post-Soviet enterprises bereft of long-established contracts with suppliers and customers. Despite the steps being taken at intergovernmental level to harmonize duties and other taxes, Uzbekistan has chosen to remain outside any customs union, while Kazakstan is committed to the close integration of the 'Four'. The governments of both republics have sponsored 'financial-industrial groups', notably with Russian enterprises and banks. The North Ust-yurt gasfield (Karakalpakstan) is being developed to supply Ukraine (eventually more than 500 million cu. m annually) and there are a number of joint ventures with enterprises elsewhere in the CIS. Among apparently successful collaborations is the Tajik-Uzbek exploitation of the Altyntopkan gold deposit which straddles the frontier of the two states.

[21] *Financial Times*, 9 April 1996.

A number of bilateral issues of economic relevance are outstanding. Most of the frontier and minority problems have an economic dimension, but among more strictly economic ones, those which still elude agreement are between Uzbekistan and Turkmenistan on the division of the rich Kokdumalak oil and gas deposit (its reserves are Uzbekistan's largest in gas and there are also 100 million tonnes of oil), which was on the agenda at the Chardzou summit of January 1996 (but, as noted above, the only accord gained was about Amu Darya water); and with Tajikistan on Uzbek gas sales (suspended in October 1995 because of Tajik non-payment) and rail tariffs charged for transit of the Tajikistan sector of the Fergana Valley.

The persistence of state enterprises, particularly in the energy sector, and their indebtedness under price control led to the accumulation of interstate debts: an agreement at prime ministerial level in early 1996 led to the reduction of Kazakstan's debts to Uzbekistan for gas from $138 million to $33.4 million (as also of its debt to Kyrgyzstan for electricity). In August 1996 Kyrgyzstan agreed terms for repayment of its two-year arrears on gas purchases from Uzbekistan, half to be settled in convertible currency and half in Kyrgyz farm produce.[22]

Transport

The first Central Asian Conference on Transport Routes was held in Almaty in May 1996: the five Central Asian states were represented at deputy minister level and there was participation from the three Caucasian states. Disputes over transport tariffs, profit distribution and transport management were aired and particular concern was expressed over the need to invest in road surfacing and in port reconstruction on the Caspian. On ports, an Uzbek delegation in April 1996 contracted with the Georgian Black Sea port of Poti for long-term facilities for Uzbek trade avoiding Russia. Transport has been a priority for the Economic Cooperation Organization (ECO), founded in 1964 by Iran, Pakistan and Turkey, and reactivated in 1992 to include the five Central Asian states, together with Afghanistan and Azerbaijan.[23] Meeting in Pakistan in March 1995, ECO set up a trade and development bank, a shipping company and airline, and a reinsurance company. On the eve of the ECO summit meeting in Ashgabat (May 1996), leaders of ECO member states and other countries gathered at Sarakhs on the Turkmen–Iranian border to inaugurate a link between the Central Asian and Iranian railway networks, with a new line to the

[22] *Central Asia Newsfile*, July 1996, p. 10.
[23] Bruno de Cordier, 'The Economic Cooperation Organization: Towards a New Silk Road on the Ruins of the Cold War?', *Central Asian Survey*, Vol. 15, No. 1, 1996, pp. 47–57; Richard Pomfret, *The Economies of Central Asia*, Princeton University Press, Princeton, NJ, 1995, pp. 158–60.

Persian Gulf port of Bandar Abbas also planned. Turkey projects a line to replace the ferry across Lake Van and hence speed rail traffic to and from Europe. Iran (which has secured Tehran as the headquarters of ECO) is making Sarakhs a free trade zone. Russia and Kazakstan signed an agreement on railway regulations during the CIS Summit in October 1996.

Tashkent airport has long been a 'hub', with Aeroflot and others offering cheap flights between western Europe and the Indian sub-continent and beyond, which Almaty was not, but both now have some (though as yet inadequate) direct long-haul links. The national airlines, which took over Aeroflot's assets in each country, are re-equipping their small fleets and Uzbekistan Airlines is buying cargo planes (IL-76) from the V. P. Chkalov Aviation Corporation, Tashkent, one of the country's promising high-technology industries. However, the national airline, Kazakstan Aue Zholy, was bankrupted in 1996 (amid allegations of excessive free ticketing and salting money in 48 bank accounts at home and abroad); the government gave part of its assets to a new company of its own, Air Kazakstan.[24] As already mentioned, Sumitomo of Japan is contracted to bring Akmola airport to international standards as it becomes the capital of Kazakstan.

But the biggest transport issue is for the international shipment of oil and gas. The markets for Kazak oil and gas are in Europe in the short run and in Asia in the longer run. In western Europe, the delivered price of gas must be competitive with supply from the North Sea, Russia and Algeria (the latter now reaching consumers via Spain as well as via Italy); projects to supply the Indian sub-continent and the Pacific Rim countries involve a great deal of capital but are attractive to economies with hydrocarbon deficits and concern for a 'clean' fossil fuel. For Kazak oil, outlets through the Black Sea, the Mediterranean and the Persian Gulf all offer access to worldwide markets.

The Caspian Pipeline Consortium (CPC) had its origin in an agreement between the Kazak and Omani governments to form a joint venture for a pipeline from Tengiz to Western markets. The interest of the government of Oman lay in its 'strong, if only partly explained, relationship' with a Bermuda-based entrepreneur of Dutch origin, John Deuss.[25] Joined shortly afterwards by the Russian government, the CPC intended to lay a pipeline to the Russian Black Sea port of Novorossiisk. Unrealistically, the owners of CPC wanted Chevron, as the customer, to contribute in non-voting shares to the cost, to which in particular the Oman Oil Company (a joint venture of Deuss with the State of Oman) would pay little for an inordinate

[24] Michael Ustugov, 'Financial Catastrophe of National Airline', *Focus Central Asia*, No. 18, 30 September 1996, pp. 17–20.
[25] McDonell, in Allison, pp. 341–4.

return. After tense negotiations, during which Chevron put its Tengiz operations on to 'care and maintenance' only, Deuss was bought out by the Omani government (January 1996) and Chevron joined CPC as a full partner. Mobil had by then already bought into Tengizchevroil (taking over half the Kazak government's shareholding) and hence was also a stakeholder, and Royal Dutch Shell participated a few weeks later by financing part of the Russian share. In March 1996, CPC was radically restructured, to the detriment of the Omani equity (reduced to 7 per cent, against 24 per cent for Russia and 19 per cent for Kazakstan) and with the participation of other oil and gas companies. Of the 50 per cent owned by oil companies, Chevron had 15 per cent and Mobil 7.5 per cent, and the remainder has been taken by LUKoil, the biggest Russian private oil firm (12.5 per cent), Rosneft-Shell (7.5), British Gas and Agip (each 2 per cent), and Munaigas (wholly state-owned in Kazakstan) and Oryx Energy (a US independent), each with 1.75 per cent. The final agreement was signed in Moscow on 6 December 1996, envisaging a cost of $2 billion and completion by 1999. Apart from the Russian government's direct holding, Rosneft is still wholly state-owned and discussions were proceeding on an equity stake for the pipeline operator, also state-owned, Transneft.[26] With Rosneft having a 51 per cent share to Shell's 49 per cent, the total Russian state holding in CPC is 44 per cent.[27] The 1,500 km pipeline would be sufficient to carry all Kazak oil exports up to the year 2015, but might also carry some Russian crude from the Emba area. From Tengiz and Emba the line crosses into Russia and links with projected supplies from Azerbaijan at Tikhoretsk to deliver oil at the port of Novorossiisk. Together with improving shipment facilities there – storms can close it for up to two months annually – the cost is estimated at between $1.2 and $1.5 billion. The problems associated with its viability include political instability in Russia, the renewal of hostilities in Chechenia, through which the line passes, the possibility that other Russian administrations might impose penal transit dues and the limits on tanker passage through the Bosporus.[28]

The genesis of the Kazakstan Pipeline Company S.A. (KPC), established in Paris, for an oil pipeline from the Kazak deposits under the Caspian Sea was a scheme of the UK/US consulting engineers Brown and Root formulated in October 1994. It foresaw transport of both Kazak and Azerbaijani oil by routeing a pipeline under the Caspian (from Aktau to Makhachkala), where it could take on Azerbaijani

[26] *Financial Times*, 7 December 1996.

[27] Sergey Stepashenko, 'Russia Controls Oil Business in Kazakstan', *Focus Central Asia*, No. 18, 30 September 1996, p. 2. But Arco (US), already in joint venture with LUKoil, plans to buy enough of LUKoil's equity to bring US companies' shares to 30 per cent (allowing them for US tax to deduct local taxation as a cost).

[28] See J. Roberts, *Caspian Pipelines*, FSS Key Paper, RIIA, London, June 1996.

crude: annual throughputs were planned at 25 million tonnes of Azerbaijani and 20 million tonnes of Kazak oil. The landfall at Makhachkala is in Russia (Dagestan), but the route would have avoided the war-torn Chechenia, and would traverse Georgia (avoiding Armenia) and proceed across Turkey to Ceyhan, or to the Black Sea at Supsa. This variant was estimated to cost $2,600 million, but if the sub-Caspian crossing were replaced by a loop around the north of the Caspian, the cost could be reduced to $2,210 million. The planned KPC landfall is no longer at Makhachkala, but near Baku, thereby avoiding any connection with Russia.

The export composition of the Karachaganak consortium (British Gas, Agip and LUKoil), from which the Kazakstan government's Kazakgaz gets 85 per cent of production, is uncertain. Condensate through the CPC to Novorossiisk has priority, with gas through Gazprom's network at a later stage. Kazakstan still has to buy gas from Uzbekistan and has been limited in sales to Russia by Gazprom's failure to accord regular space on its pipelines. To diminish this dependence there are plans to lay a line from the Caspian littoral to the Chimkent pipeline, collecting crude from Kumkol *en route*.[29]

Personal travel

Tashkent, Bukhara and Samarkand had been reinstated on Intourist's visitable list under Khrushchev's policy of 'peaceful co-existence' and token groups of Central Asian Muslims were allowed to make the *haj*. With no political barrier, tourism offers substantial prospects for foreign-exchange earnings. History has endowed Uzbekistan somewhat better than Kazakstan, and a Presidential Decree of June 1995 laid down a series of measures for developing this potential, especially in Bukhara, Khiva, Samarkand and Tashkent. Everywhere hotel accommodation is still inadequate in quantity and quality, but is improving. Mountaineering, skiing, caving and desert trekking offer scope for foreign earnings, and the recently established rail linkages from Kazakstan into China and prospectively from Uzbekistan, via Turkmenistan, to the Persian Gulf allow long-distance tourist travel across thousands of miles of Asia. The pilgrimage to Mecca is unrestricted and governments have been helpful in arranging mass travel. Both countries have places of pilgrimage for incoming Muslims, in Uzbekistan the tomb of Imam Bukhari near Samarkand and in Kazakstan a noted mausoleum in the town of Turkestan.

---

[29] Details of these and other pipelines are in Kairgel'dy Kabyldin, Anatoli Lobaev and Klara Rakhmetova, 'Kazakstan Oil in the Central Asian, Russian and World Context', *Kazakhstan i Mirovoe Soobshchestvo*, No. 3, 1995, pp. 11–19.

Participation in the international agencies

Fresh from a partnership agreement with the presidents of the three other Central Asian states, Presidents Karimov and Nazarbayev celebrated the entry of their countries into the United Nations in March 1992; shortly afterwards the two states joined most other agencies in the UN family. A recent Uzbek review of this relationship[30] drew particular attention to UNICEF, UNESCO, UNITAR, UNDP, UNHCR, UNIDO, UNCTAD, WHO, UNFPA and WMO,[31] agencies of especial concern to a developing country.

As already mentioned, Kazakstan in July 1992 and Uzbekistan in September 1992 were accepted into the International Monetary Fund, and immediately thereafter into the World Bank (with quotas of $386 million and $294 million respectively), and their affiliates, the International Development Association (IDA) and the International Finance Corporation. They have observer status in the World Trade Organization and both are applying to become full members, although membership is not granted automatically. Both are members of the IAEA, ICAO, ITU, UPU and WIPO.[32]

An intergovernmental agreement on combating traffic in illegal narcotics was signed by ministers of the five Central Asian states and the Executive Director of the United Nations Narcotics Control Board in May 1996. Uzbekistan has an intergovernmental agreement with Kazakstan on cooperation in the suppression of tax fraud (May 1996); the Uzbek State Tax Committee and the Tax Inspectorate of Kazakstan are the executive authorities.

Among regional organizations both countries are members of two UN regional commissions, the Economic and Social Commission for Asia and the Pacific (ESCAP), and the Economic Commission for Europe (as are all Soviet successor states[33]), and founder-members of the European Bank for Reconstruction and Development, the *Transition Report* of which is a main source of international comment on their economies. The EBRD Vice-President, attending the opening of

---

[30] In the Tashkent *Narodnoe slovo*, 23 April 1996.

[31] Respectively, the UN's Children's Fund; Educational, Scientific and Cultural Organization; Institute for Training and Reseach; Development Programme; High Commissioner for Refugees; Industrial Development Organization; Conference on Trade and Development; World Health Organization; UN Fund for Population Activities; World Meteorological Organization.

[32] Respectively, International Atomic Energy Agency; International Civil Aviation Organization; International Telecommunication Union; Universal Postal Union; World Intellectual Property Organization. A symposium on assistance to transition countries (with papers on the IMF, World Bank, EBRD, EU, UN and UNIDO) is in *Most: Economic Policy in Transitional Economies,* Vol. 5, No. 2, 1995, pp. 85–252.

[33] That membership ensures that the Secretariat's analysis in its annual *Economic Survey of Europe* looks at the CIS as a group, whereas all other international agencies treat the countries separately.

the Uzbek gold development which his Bank was backing, warned that member states were statutorily committed to the 'fundamental principle of multi-party democracy, the rule of law, respect for human rights and market economics'. Kazakstan's Agreement on Partnership and Cooperation with the European Union awaits ratification, but Uzbekistan is not quite as far advanced; the TACIS Programme has provided much assistance to each; and both have signed the EU's Energy Charter.[34]

[34] On CIS involvement in the European Energy Charter, see Martyn Nicholls and Henry Potter, 'Regional Initiatives in the Former Soviet Bloc', *Communist Economies and Economic Transformation*, Vol. 6, No. 3, 1994, pp. 135–40.

5 CONCLUSIONS

By comparison with most other Union Republics, the economies of Kazakstan and Uzbekistan seem to have gained more from, and were less distorted by, the Soviet system. The resource in which they were particularly abundant, labour, was enhanced both in quantity and quality, with clear benefits for human development and social relations. The Soviet system broke the power of landlords over the peasantry, freed women for gainful employment and provided a choice of occupation. The system improved the quality of the workforce by assuring literacy; by providing opportunity for secondary, further and tertiary education; and by making health care widely available. Productive equipment and infrastructure were installed to derive added value from the region's natural resources. Popular attitudes remained more open to the profit motive and were hence quickly receptive to marketization at the level of the bazaar and small enterprise.

To suggest such gains is not to belittle the coercion, mortality and disruptions that accompanied the imposition of such changes. Rather, it stresses the value of the base upon which the new system can build. The changeover has been deliberately gradual, but as macroeconomic stability takes the place of the repressed inflation of the past and the open inflation after the 1992 'shock', a market-oriented reform of institutions is being undertaken.

The restructuring of the economy currently under way has two main dimensions. The productive profile is being adapted from protected exchanges within a command economy to a competitive pattern of output. In terms of international relations, 1995 was a landmark for Uzbekistan as the first year in which exports to former Soviet states fell below half the total. Its cotton exports and Kazakstan's metals have been opened towards competitive hard-currency markets and are attracting external enterprise, capital and technology. It is recognized that both agricultural and industrial techniques must be adapted to render them environmentally more benign, notably for water supply (including those needed to reverse depletion of the Aral Sea), and to enhance labour intensity (as agrarian overpopulation is reduced). In both republics manufacturing is at the forefront of change – much helped by new joint ventures. As these raise the productivity of capital, rural labour is being shifted out of agriculture without migration to towns; for political as well as economic reasons, the two governments and their international advisers stress the creation of small businesses. Privatization is all but complete in that sector (as also for housing), but the adaptation to its incentives and efficiency in large state enterprises is being conducted in tandem with foreign companies, the state retaining equity through management contracts or in joint ventures. Some industrial branches are reserved for full state ownership, but it remains to be seen whether such fencing off will be permanent.

Much restructuring is being required – as throughout the transition economies – after privatization or absorption into foreign ownership. Some of the corresponding investment will come from abroad – private capital and official assistance including loans from the EBRD and the World Bank Group. But most must originate in domestic savings, and (as stressed in Chapter 2) the banks should be equal to the function of gathering and efficiently distributing those funds. Public infrastructure will patently also need public investment, and in Kazakstan a large cost will fall on the government in making Akmola a suitable capital city. Foreign participation is already involved: the UK is contributing to the building and equipping of a large hospital (to cost in all $62.5 million) and the Japanese Sumitomo Company is reconstructing Akmola airport.

Three trends are embodied in external economic strategy. The first is import substitution – embracing greater food self-sufficiency, and fostering new products for which a substantial home market could be promoted or where recent import penetration could reasonably be reduced by competitive home goods. Import penetration has greatly risen in textiles and clothing, and a policy has been adopted in Uzbekistan of enhancing value-added in cotton and silk. In the Soviet period only 20 per cent of cotton was domestically absorbed, and foreign investment is entering the weaving and garment-making sectors, hopefully both for export and retail sale.[1]

The second trend is the attraction of foreign investment into oil, gas and metal export lines, which will principally benefit Kazakstan. Uzbekistan's main export commodity is not only on a trend of declining production but will face stiffer world competition. A study by the Dutch Rabobank forecasts against the current 20 million tonnes a world cotton crop of 21.4 million tonnes in the year 2000, most of the increment coming from higher yields (and hence probably cheaper).[2]

The third trend is reduction of the invisibles deficit, by the creation of domestic financial services capable of external transaction and by the encouragement of leisure facilities for both domestic and tourist users. Foreign investors have a key political as well as economic role in this strategy and they need to be assured of equi-

[1] Saanat Wachidowa, 'Economic Reform and Restructuring in Uzbekistan', in Heribert Dieter (ed.), *Regionale Integration in Zentralasien*, Metropolis, Marburg, 1996, pp. 295–302.
[2] *The World Cotton Complex*, Rabobank International (reported in *Financial Times*, 21 November 1996).

table economic conditions and political stability. Though much has been done on market-protective law and practice, the bureaucracy does not always give enterprise a fair wind. Particularly trenchant comments have been made in a recent study addressed to business interests. On Uzbekistan an equity analyst of a leading international investment bank wrote: 'Reform will progress as the product of interaction between the actions of the President, who has sole control of the policy agenda, and the day-to-day actions of bureaucrats within sectoral ministries'[3] on Kazakstan the Director of the Kazakstan-UK Centre warned that 'although theoretically a foreign investor can have recourse to the courts, the majority realistically forgo taking this route, for it is too unreliable, inefficient and effectively subservient to higher authorities ... it will be a waste of time, especially if it is the tax inspectorate or customs which is being challenged.'[4] A lesson still to be fully absorbed from the medieval Silk Road is the mutual respect and dependence of trader and ruler.

---

[3] James Wood (employing bank unstated), 'Uzbekistan', in Martin McCauley (ed.), *Investing in the Caspian Sea Region*, p. 85.
[4] Gregory Andrusz, 'Kazakstan', in ibid., p. 46.

FURTHER READING

Current statistics and informed comment on the economy have been available for Kazakstan since the beginning of 1996 in the quarterly *Kazakstan Economic Trends*, with *Monthly Updates*, prepared jointly by the Centre for Economic Reform (of the Government of Kazakstan) and the European Expertise Service (financed by the EU's TACIS Programme). Publication of *Uzbekistan Economic Trends* is scheduled for the spring of 1997. Footnote references in this study indicate the range of data and analysis presented in publications of international organizations of which the two republics are members – notably the UN, IMF, World Bank and EBRD. The OECD has published *Investment Guide for Uzbekistan* (with UNDP) and a regular series, *Trends and Policies in Privatisation*. The Statistical Committees of the CIS, of Kazakstan and of Uzbekistan publish annual and other abstracts (as also cited in footnotes); these are in Russian, but that from Uzbekistan has a parallel text in English; summaries of economic developments in all CIS states are in the monthly *Ekonomika i politika Rossii i gosudarstv Blizhnego Zarubezhh'ya* of IMEMO, Moscow. The Economist Intelligence Unit produces a quarterly *Country Report* on *Kazakstan* and on *Kyrgyz Republic, Tajikistan, Turkmenistan, Uzbekistan*; from First Quarter 1997, there will be a separate *Uzbekistan* Report; it also circulates a quarterly *Country Risk Service*. *Abstracts: Russian and East European Series (ABREES)* publishes quarterly about twenty summaries of articles in Kazak and Uzbek newspapers and journals and there is coverage of the two republics in *Financial Times East European Energy Report* and in *Russia Express*, published by International Industrial Information Ltd. BBC Monitoring publishes a weekly newsletter, *Inside Central Asia*, presenting selected media reports, covered in more detail in its *Summary of World Broadcasts*, Part 1, *Former USSR*. *Kazakstan Survey* is published in Almaty and Washington, DC by the International Tax and Investment Center; *Caspian Brief*, published by Arguments and Facts Media of Hastings, contains reports on Kazak affairs and *Focus Central Asia: Analytical Report*, published in London and Almaty, has journalistic briefs on all five states. Finally, the Central Asia Research Forum of the London University School of Oriental and African Studies publishes monthly *Central Asia Newsfile* and quarterly *Labyrinth*.

Among many recent books on the region, attention may particularly be drawn to:

Allison, Roy (ed.), *Challenges for the Former Soviet South*, Brookings Institution Press, Washington, DC, for Royal Institute of International Affairs.

Allworth, Edward (ed.), *Central Asia: 130 Years of Russian Dominance, A Historical Overview*, 3rd edn, Duke University Press, Durham, NC and London, 1994.

Dyker, David A. (ed.), *Investment Opportunities in Russia and the CIS,* Brookings Institution Press, Washington, DC, for RIIA.

Forsythe, Rosemarie, *The Politics of Oil in the Caucasus and Central Asia*, Adelphi Paper No. 300, 1996, Oxford University Press, Oxford, for IISS.

Gleason, Gregory, *The Central Asian States: Discovering Independence*, Westview, Boulder, CO, forthcoming April 1997.

Hiro, Dilip, *Between Marx and Muhammad: The Changing Face of Central Asia,* HarperCollins, London, 1994.

Hunter, Shireen T., *Central Asia since Independence*, Praeger, Westport, CT, 1996.

Kulchik, Yuri, Andrey Fadin and Victor Sergeev, *Central Asia after the Empire*, Pluto Press, London, 1996.

McAuley, Martin (ed.), *Investing in the Caspian Sea Region*, Cartermill, London, 1996.

Mesbahi, Mohiadin (ed.), *Central Asia and the Caucasus after the Soviet Union*, University Press of Florida, Gainsville, FL, 1994.

Pomfret, Richard, *The Economies of Central Asia*, Princeton University Press, Princeton, NJ, 1995.

Pomfret, Richard, *Asian Economies in Transition: Reforming Centrally Planned Economies,* Edward Elgar, Cheltenham, 1996.

Rumer, Boris (ed.), *Central Asia in Transition: Dilemmas of Political and Economic Development*, M. E. Sharpe, Armonk, NY and London.

A list of relevant studies in the RIIA Former Soviet South series is on p. 74 and on the back cover of this paper.

Published Former Soviet South Papers

Turkey in Post-Soviet Central Asia
Gareth Winrow (Bosphorus University)
Analyses the evolution of Turkish political and economic involvement in the Central Asian states from the enthusiasm and optimism of 1991-2 to the realism of the mid-1990s.

Iran and the Former Soviet South
Edmund Herzig (RIIA)
An examination of Iran's political, economic and ideological interests in the new states across its northern borders and their responses.

The Russian Policy Debate on Central Asia
Irina Zviagelskaia (Russian Centre for Strategic Research & International Studies)
Focuses on the main strands of thinking and the principal actors and interest groups influencing Russian policy towards Central Asia.

Rural and Agricultural Development in Uzbekistan
Peter Craumer (Florida International University)
Considers the economic, social and environmental factors in contemporary Uzbekistan's rural development and their effects on the economy and society of the country as a whole.

The Formation of Kazakh Identity: From Tribe to Nation-State
Shirin Akiner (SOAS, London University)
A study of the fusion of various elements in the formation of contemporary Kazakh identity, which also sets this process in the broader context of post-Soviet nation-building.

Georgia: From Chaos to Stability?
Jonathan Aves (Sussex University)
Analyses Georgia's recent progress towards a more secure and stable statehood.

Caspian Pipelines
John Roberts (Middle East Consultants)
Assesses the pros and cons of the various projects for pipelines to bring Caspian oil and gas resources to world markets.

CIS Integration Trends: Russia and the Former Soviet South
Mark Webber (Loughborough University)
Examines the progress towards integration in the CIS and its significance for the Central Asian and Caucasian countries.

The Economies of Kazakstan and Uzbekistan
Michael Kaser (Birmingham University)
A comparative analysis of the economies and economic policy of the two largest Central Asian states.

Ordering Information

UK and Rest of Europe
Plymbridge Distributors
Tel (+44) (0)1752 202 301
Fax (+44) (0)1752 202 333

For US, Canada and Rest of World
The Brookings Institution
1 800 275 1447 or 202 797 6258
202 707 6004